THE HALLELUJAH SHADOW

THE HALLELUJAH SHADOW

ESSAYS

ANDREW SANT

PUNCHER & WATTMANN

in association with Shoestring Press, UK

First published in 2020
Published by Puncher and Wattmann
PO Box 279
Waratah NSW 2298

http://www.puncherandwattmann.com
puncherandwattmann@bigpond.com

NATIONAL
LIBRARY
OF AUSTRALIA

A catalogue entry for this book is available from the National Library of Australia.

ISBN   9781925780840
Printed by Lightning Source International

This project has been assisted by the Australian Government through the Australia Council, its arts funding and advisory body.

Australian Government

ACKNOWLEDGEMENTS

'On Being Sincere' was first published in *Southerly* (Vol. 78 No. 2) in 2018.

'On Getting Lost' was first published in *Island* (No. 150) in 2017.

'On Looking into Mirrors' was first published in *Griffith Review* (No. 68) in 2020.

'On Mortality' was first published in *Southerly* (Vol. 78 No. 2) in 2018.

'On Regret' was first published in *Meanjin* (Vol. 77, No. 1) in 2018.

'On the Record' was first published in *Island* (No. 157) in 2019.

'On Settling Down' was first published in *Island* (No. 150) in 2017.

'On Swimming in the Sea' appeared as a *Meanjin* blog in October 2017.

'On Writing', part 1 of 'On Concentration: Writing and Reading' was first published in *Collected* online (Royal Literary Fund) in July 2017.

ABOUT THE AUTHOR

Andrew Sant was born in London. He emigrated with his parents to Melbourne where he completed his education. He has subsequently lived in London at various times, including much of the last decade. During this time was Writing Fellow at the Universities of Leicester, Chichester and London (Goldsmiths College) and Kent. In 2001 he was writer-in-residence at the University of Peking in Beijing, China. He jointly founded and edited for ten years the Tasmanian-based quarterly, *Island*. Parallel occupations have included work as a teacher, copywriter and arts consultant. He is a former member of the Literature Board of the Australia Council. Among the most recent of his twelve collections of poetry are *The Bicycle Thief & Other Poems* (Black Pepper, 2013) and *Baffling Gravity* (Shoestring Press/Puncher & Wattmann, 2019). His essays have appeared in the annual *Best Australian Essays* anthology and in the   collection *How to Proceed* (Shoestring Press/Puncher & Wattmann, 2016). In 2003 he was awarded the Centenary Medal by the Australian Government. He now lives in Melbourne.

For Tina

CONTENTS

On Regret 1

On Getting Lost 7

On Concentration: Writing and Reading 13

On Swimming in the Sea 21

On Settling Down 25

On Sight 31

On Getting the Unexpected 35

On the Hallelujah and Other Shadows 41

On Bothering to Travel 45

On Being Sincere 51

On Looking into Mirrors 55

On Memory 59

On the Record 65

On Smoking and Social Atomisation 75

On Mortality 79

On the Future 85

ON REGRET

'Regrets I've had a few/But then again too few to mention', the famous song declares. It is enduringly popular: the singer did it his way. This hymn to individualism I heard broadcast the other day to us shoppers, one familiar song following another, in a place of conformity and predictability, a large supermarket, where occasionally a distracted customer, oblivious to others, will sing along or hum. I didn't—I'm reasonably sure—in that somnambulistic state generated by supermarkets, as shoppers drift down one aisle after another, sing snatches of 'My Way' but I did, masked no doubt by an expressionless face, wonder about regret.

There must be categories of regret, ranging from the severe to the trivial, just a few severe ones, too few to mention, perhaps easily dismissed along the highway of going my way. Next song, please. It was raining when I exited the supermarket and I regretted not bringing my fold-up umbrella. Trivial, too, a thousand other regrets, though not immediately, say, amid a downpour, the heavens grumpy with thunder. The voice raised in anger, the uncharitable act, the parked car, one's own, with the keys left in the ignition, stolen, then the consequence: regret. Murder might not easily qualify for the regrets too few to mention—for, that is, a repentant murderer. The other guy, the deceased, has run out of manifold opportunities for regret most of which, thankfully, and in the interests of waking up in the morning with the prospect of a fair day ahead, flicker a bit then fade. Making room, I suppose, for the next bunch of regrets, a common feature, from the severe to the trivial, surely being that someone who regrets something must be the agent of that regret. It can't be inflicted upon him: the world may seem a terrible place but that's not a cause for regret; the fact that he personally contributed to this situation might well be should he happen to pass judgement on the matter.

It follows, possibly, that such a person might regret being born. Since hearing—once again, once too often, individualism being rampant—Frank Sinatra skating over his regrets, the big ones maybe, the ones most people can't hum along to, I've paused to consider my own regrets, the trivial too many to mention and mainly forgotten. But how about any up the scale that are outstanding? Sorrows, yes, certainly they have hung around since they generate themselves—if, incidentally, Paul Anka, who wrote 'My Way' had written 'sorrows' instead of 'regrets' the song's authority would have been compromised, try singing it and see—and in our transient, mortal lives they are the common, regular lot. Regrets? I am not a repentant murderer though I have felt murderous, inclined towards justifiable homicide; have been rash, bad, a cad, myriad things I might not be glad to find in others, a sporadic hypocrite therefore, and thus a fine, sometimes desperate, example of a man born to be flawed—indeed a man who once owned a dog, still the subject, decades later, of abject regret.

It is one thing to treat another human being casually—did Neville Chamberlain on behalf of his fellow countrymen and women come to regret appeasing Adolf Hitler?—quite another so to treat a dog. The name I gave her was Almost. She almost died—hence her name—the day or days after I spontaneously bought her, rescued her, as I valiantly saw it, from a stall dealing in pets at a large inner-city market. The stallholder lifted her out of a cage from among the rest of the weeks-old litter, I parted with some cash from my gardening round—this was back in my student days—carried the warm pup, which made high-pitched sounds that did not yet qualify as barks, to my old VW, which barely qualified as being roadworthy, wherein, soon after I drove off, the pup threw up. There seemed to be more vomit on the floor of the car, undigested offal, than dog. The quivering little creature, wide-eyed with fear, had been starved then stuffed to be made to look more robust. This was a poor start to a dynamic master and dog relationship. My live-in girlfriend, who was with me, witnessed it, and this was fortunate, indeed there was no arguing—at least in respect to this unexpected situation—about the fact that the yet-to-be named pup would, if she was to survive, benefit from the attentions of a team rather than a single person to which, in the days following, gravely intestinal, we added a vet.

The pup lived to respond to her name. Almost was predominantly a kelpie and, at this stage, her every sharp, sensitive instinct would have told her that her master was up to the job. I walked her, I fed her, I trained her. When I left inner-city Melbourne to live in outlying country she, sitting obediently in the back seat of the car, came with me. I regretted, for her sake, I had not done it earlier. Almost! I'd call, masterfully, Almost! Almost! and she'd appear immediately, ears pricked, run towards me away from some secondary business, probably olfactory. There was a consistency in our relationship, a lack of high drama, decidedly missing in the parallel relationship I had with my girlfriend, no longer live-in, which frequently took me well away from my studies in a way that a long walk with Almost—no lead, across paddocks, through bushland, startling kangaroos, all the while being wary for both of us, since it was summer, of snakes—simply did not. There's a reason why there are countless individuals out on the streets, in parkland, anywhere, walking dogs, talking to them. I regretted some of the things I said to my girlfriend, maybe she equally regretted some stunning things she said to me—we had a significant, dynamic capacity to generate possible regret. Act first, regret later was our unofficial slogan. For which we had a shared responsibility, as in any such relationship. Double the responsibility to the full 100 per cent for the committed owner of a dog.

The photograph, black and white, now forty years old, I still have of Almost, though not, as a constant reminder of her, on view, shows her sitting on her haunch looking up at the camera, at me. Her look, in spite of the strange mechanical object, a Minolta reflex, I am holding to my eye, is one of absolute trust. Her forepaws are white, her legs fine, her fur parti-coloured, brown and white if the photo had been taken in colour. She was small for a kelpie, perhaps because of her wretched start in life. In her movements, briskly running about in open spaces or trotting along beside me, she was elegant. When daily I returned from university to the self-contained outhouse, which I'd rented on a farm, and released her from a long leash—there were cattle and other hoofed animals around to whom she might have been tempted to give some genetically bred-in bother—she would, there seems no more accurate word for it, dance, on her hind legs, her

3

tail wagging heart-fast, and I'd hold her forepaws, reaching up to me, in mutual greeting.

A surprised onlooker would have observed a man and a dog perform a jig. That dog, born on the wrong side of the tracks, was naturally refined: her face was symmetrically white around the nose and drew attention to her dark, alert eyes. Those eyes that again looked up at me with complete trust after, exhausted and vulnerable, she'd given birth to a litter of six—the scent of a bitch on heat can travel for miles so there must have been many eager contenders in the region, beyond my knowledge, to sire them—for, well, five of them, weeks later, delivery to exceptionally good (vetted) homes where refinement in a dog did not necessarily correspond to the snobbish need for pedigree. The sixth pup we kept—another lovely bitch to love.

Memory is the location of regret. It is capacious. The farm didn't need to be large. Memories inspire tunes in the minor key, the sad one. If I could play the fiddle, it now might be appropriate in the course of this recalling of events to angle the bow and begin to play such a tune, preparatory, in A minor, to be specific, as if after years of practice. Get out maybe, like those guys one sees playing bagpipes in unlikely places, who seem to like nothing better than to stroll out into the dark, an open space, moonlit or misty for effect, and play, plaintively, to no other audience, unless inadvertently, than the night air. Doing it their way.

However, right now there's another thing it pains me to recall, insists on a hearing, and therefore that I move on as a dog does from an excused bone: Almost was fiercely loyal. It seemed to be her version of a vocation. Of course her complex, unique interior life was beyond me—my attempt to do her justice now is in spite of this—but a matter that was serially evident emerged when someone she perceived to be a stranger approached me, a possible threat, an agent of the unexpected. She would bare her teeth and snarl, ready to defend. Then, since I assumed I wasn't about to be shot or mugged, I'd signal to her, firmly, to withdraw her best of intentions, back off from frightening an innocent party which, judging from the activity of her tail and the relaxation of her ears, came as a significant relief during those times given to constant vigilance when we were at large, off the farm.

Then once again we moved on. This was further up country both in distance and altitude. Three of us now, the two dogs and me, a cohesive little pack in which each member knew his or her place, the dogs' loyalty genes in top working order. I led us in my old set of wheels to a fibro shack surrounded by bush, ticking in the summer heat that day. When I was at work nearby, labouring—indisputably not what a university degree had prepared me for but I knew my place, at a remove well north of where the degree was earned—I generally left the dogs, once we'd settled in, as lookouts, sentinels, defenders, each to her own particular place on the rented property. On my daily return, there was confirmation. At such times in their young lives they were suddenly meteors circling the shack and, boy, could they also leap and yelp to let a leader know that he was needed.

The day I came home and they were nowhere to be found was wickedly hot. In place of the dogs stood the bush, a presence, withheld, silent, in a lull. My enquiries went beyond there. Days later I found them lying together, Almost and her pale grey and white progeny whom I'd called Sprout, under the shack, hidden away, where they'd gone in agony to die, dogs being the most correct of creatures. I hadn't reckoned on the locals laying fox baits. My charges' vigilance had not been returned. I couldn't more completely have let them down. The dogs I have since taken for walks, taken to a beach or park, looked after, fed, thrown a bone to, patted and played with, none have been my own. I own a deep regret. It dogs me to this day.

ON GETTING LOST

A bee is zipping about inside a moving car—or crawling up the misted window. Its behaviour is unpredictable. The bee, used to taking its bearings from the angle of the sun, is probably disorientated. It might sting the driver of the car or one of his passengers. One or possibly all of them likely know that if a beekeeper shifts a hive even a short distance, members of the colony react by flying fast and furiously to and from the original position of the hive to where it has been moved. The bees' mood has switched from workaday composure to that of alarm. One of those passengers in the car insisted, in this story I was recently told, that the trapped bee immediately have its freedom restored— that the speeding car be brought to a halt. What makes the story striking and now worth relating is that the passenger—a lawyer, as it happens—did not demand an immediate rather than eventual cessation of vehicular movement because he or one of his fellow passengers, as anyone might predict, could be stung. His concern therefore seeming to be about human safety, especially his own. Not at all. His concern was for the worker bee. Specifically, that the bee might, after it had been driven too many kilometres, get lost and no longer be able to locate her hive. How likely and complicated for her this might have been I do not know. To be plain, it's the thought that counts. To, in addition, admire the thought, it was not one that in nearly every case verging on all cases would have been foremost in the minds of a bunch of urban travellers speeding in a car with an energetic and fully equipped bee inside, complete with modified ovipositor, the stinging bit. The lawyer won his marvellous argument and the car quickly pulled over to the side of the road where the bee was set free.

How possible is it for a bee to get lost? How readily is it possible for us humans to get lost? We know it happens. We don't like the prospect. If we live in a city, there are signposts everywhere. If we live in the country, the signposts are, with luck, judiciously placed. Wherever we live, we've initially scoped the place and, in ever widening circles, got to know the neighbourhood. If you're

7

a bee, a worker bee, you'll have been on the lookout for the best pollen in the region resulting in, most likely, a zig-zag route to find it, then a more sharply directed return to the hive where you will perform a short communicative dance to let your fellow workers know—a hive being a supremely collaborative effort—exactly along which beeline the pollen exists. Bees are good at directions. Unless perhaps they've been trapped in a moving car. The driver of that car, knowing of his or her propensity to get lost, may be making use of GPS navigation. The new ubiquity of this handy audio-visual device for idiots is testimony to the ease with which people fear they might get lost. Possibility: high. Maps, remember, have only been with us for a few hundred years, the early spatial approximations emerging out of the mists and murk of time into a clarified light where cartographic accuracy can let a person know exactly where they stand—at least in relation to something else, not necessarily comforting, a bleak hill or a hollow for instance, distant or nearby. There's no gainsaying that Aboriginal songlines, anywhere between latitudes 10° and 40° south—approximately—that is, a vast space for a human on foot to comprehend, were and are a very superior vehicle for conveying life-preserving directions. More in tune with eager, clever bees than the technologically swamped driver doomed to get lost without a GPS.

To be lost, to be extremely lost and fear the unknown consequences, is unlikely for those adults living in comfortable circumstances and who do not travel independently in foreign countries—I can attest that parts of Mandarin-speaking China for a non-speaker of Mandarin are good for getting some first-hand experience—or who don't trek somewhere off the beaten track without good sense, a decent map or, indeed, with a map to then carelessly misread. I have no attendant direct experience of how possible it is for a novice sailor to disappear for good. Failing these possibilities, it's always possible to get psychologically rather than physically lost. I favour the latter position since in extremis the lost mind will have little to offer in the way of succour or sustenance, seemingly endlessly, and experience a surfeit of arid mental thunder. To recognize the condition of being lost is, in an impressive way, to assert the value and need to feel found, so often

8

taken for granted. Being lost has an affinity with being trapped in so far as the person (or bee) in that unwelcome situation is, unless hopelessly doomed, keen to be rescued, released from the terror—urgency, surely, a more pressing factor in the desire to be saved from entrapment than from being lost. Neither, later on, quick to be forgotten.

It's remarkably easy to get lost. I found this out—unforgettably—about twenty-five years ago while camping and walking with two friends in a remote area of the Tasmanian Highlands, known as the Walls of Jerusalem. We were there in mid-autumn definitely, to be belatedly frank, a foolish time of the year to become exposed to the highland elements. Back then we were casually confident about our excursion; others had more sense. There were no other tents than our tent next to the chilly windrippled lake where, well-exercised from walking, humping the equipment and food, we made camp. Then the three of us decided on an exploratory investigation of the area, noting various alpine species of vegetation, in particular varieties of heath; pencil pines were common sentinels in the sweeping landscape with its broad depressions and high ridges. All of the species well-adapted to sub-zero temperatures. The afternoon was well advanced when the two of us who had taken the lead noticed the trailing, botanically absorbed, third member was no longer to be seen on the track, indisputably boggy, which the area of scrub we had newly entered and pushed through tended to close over. There is an accepted rule among bushwalkers which states members of a group, for reasons of safety, should always stay together. We broke this rule with distinction. After some backtracking, the two of us, unable to find the third, split up to enlarge the area of search. We had entered, up there in the Tasmanian Highlands, the realms of the lost.

One map among three walkers, and in these circumstances, is wildly insufficient. The problem as it now presented itself was somewhat phenomenological: which or all of us, and in what way, had become lost? Where, someone without a map might say—in a strange place, possibly the outer regions of space—where the fuck am I? I can verify the appropriateness of such a question as

9

cold temperatures drop further, a steady light rain turns to driven sleet and I discover I'm amidst a wide expanse of tall button grass rooted in soggy peat, wallabies hopping away this way and that as giant frogs might, and before me an impressive view of an endless undulating wilderness beginning to disappear in the dusk. I was, as they say, in a spot. Lost in physical space, without weatherproof clothing or shelter, matches or food, and lost to those who, I dared to assume, might wish to locate me.

There are many people who, during the course of our individual lives, become lost to us, possibly within a metropolis, possibly, after an emotional breach or an exceptional disagreement, with relief—the common form of getting lost. Get lost! It's a savage imperative. Wife to husband, perhaps, in the marital home: getting lost doesn't necessarily require a shift to a fresh latitudinal and longitudinal co-ordinate. Just to a basement in the family home, perhaps. I suddenly had plenty of time to think about the finer points of getting lost while lost in the Tasmanian Highlands. Was it, by now, a one-, two- or a three-way matter? If one of us wasn't lost, where exactly was the co-ordinate in that great landscape which proved that he wasn't? Was there a tent on it? These questions, in succession, might suggest that my response to the situation was a form of panic. In fact, sensing my own doom, death from exposure—known in the area—a calm, preposterous voice in my head repeated 'what a waste, what a waste', presumably referring to all manner of worthy and/ or wonderful things I could offer the world, like being a good father, but that it now would be denied. The local, vast version of nature's indifference to those sentient beings, on this occasion a forty-year old man and a number of jittery wallabies, who nevertheless must depend upon what nature provides, didn't encourage or discourage hope in me. If any encouragement was provided it was my own: I was surprised by how composed I was, this being I suppose a sensible, evolutionary response to certain kinds of danger. I may well have recalled, completely out of proportion to the then present circumstances, Apsley Cherry-Garrard's account in *The Worst Journey in the World* of his team's survival, during a long trek early last century, in the most extreme conditions in Antarctica, to gather Emperor penguins' eggs for scientific research. While I was thinking about my own next move north, south, east or west, a spin the bottle matter if I'd had one on hand, I heard a voice faintly calling from within the dim, darkening distance. I recognized it and yelled back. Some while later, beside the tent, next to a fire, I was once again with my two companions, and in effect this was as reassuring as, later next day, being back at my home address—or any other infinitely variable safe distance from getting lost.

ON CONCENTRATION: WRITING AND READING

1

Suddenly there's the obliterating sound of a banging jackhammer endeavouring to penetrate the bitumen on the road outside. Your rates or taxes inconveniently at work: silence being trashed. Or, in a conjoined house, even though it's still morning, a time for birdsong not rock music, the new neighbours have turned up their old stereo player to high, possibly for a party, so that the bass line of the song has real and deep definition, and the lyrics, familiar to you from several decades ago, are now again irresistibly clear. These are occasions when a writer, if, like me, he or she uses a pencil to make a first draft, lays it aside and hangs his head gloomily over the page and, in lone and isolated protest, curses the ubiquity of noise pollution in the contemporary world.

Have any writers, I wonder, unwittingly found themselves to be living under the flight path for a nearby international airport? This would be reason to snap countless pencils, at regular intervals, in two. An ice-cream vendor directly out the front of the house, mid-summer, advertising its cheerful arrival with jangly tunes to the children of the well-populated neighbourhood, would be another, though less chronic, reason. There may be many impediments to engaging in the writing life: enemies. Cyril Connolly, way back, identified the pram in the hall, an observation one might have expected to come more swiftly from the other side of the gender divide. I recently read a brisk interview with an urban writer in which he breezily claimed the only thing that prevents him writing is the phone ringing. I'd like to know on which quiet acre he lives and if possible move there—and inform him to his advantage that it's considerably easier to disconnect a phone than to scare off on one's own, hopelessly, an ice cream van surrounded by happy children.

Perhaps the major enemy, procrastination—which in my experience so far respects no borders—doesn't show up at his place either. It's astonishing how interesting and necessary to wash a pile of assorted crockery can become when there's writing of some kind to accomplish. Or else weeds to be kept in check. Or websites to peruse. Or, you name it, and it will be sufficient to get between—polished your shoes lately?—a writer and his desk. Should this clever, ever-to-be-replenished menace be thwarted— today I deviated helplessly for five plus cups of tea with added ginger, honey and lemon on the way to my desk—the question is, what are the optimum conditions in which to write? This is a question that can only be answered in relation to a day when the serious writer, perhaps identifying her work with the fluid identity of the nation, isn't engaged in some other activity—paid work— which provides a regular stream of income to subsidise the writing. And possibly feed a family. There can be many impediments to making writing progress and sometimes, it seems, nearly everything, a sensible day out in the sun, for instance.

But let's now assume there's a desk, paper, pencil, a sturdy chair and, sitting on it, a writer. Ready. If that writer happens to be me I have a very high preference for day to day predictability (though not in the writing) and quietness, indeed silence, which from acquaintance and knowledge of other writers are not necessary and universal requirements—otherwise much of value would never have been written—but neither are they uncommon. Anyway, they happen to be my modest requirements. Turbulence, an earthquake actual or psychological, is out. A period in prison, short, in solitary confinement, wouldn't be all that bad tucked away from the prevalence of contemporary distractions. Something else I don't want is a room to write in with an interesting and broad window view where shifting weather patterns can be readily observed or, if the room is in the city, diverse and rapid activity followed on the street below. To write is to withdraw. It isn't easy. It may not always be possible to get this across to household companions, should there be any, who in all probability won't have experienced the same pressing commitment, when they boldly call up the stairs for help of some minor but urgent kind, to an unfinished long sweeping sentence, subordinate clauses and all.

I once wrote a short poem in an unfamiliar house at a table in a room where my two female companions, sitting on a couch, were talking. Once. Long ago. A dozen lines only, published in my first book. Otherwise, goodness knows how many lines later, I've never endeavoured to repeat that performance, always thereafter in as much privacy as it's possible to assemble, sometimes under tricky circumstances, and in dwellings too numerous to mention. How any of my colleagues, those who are not journalists, manage to write poems or stories in cafes, when not out of necessity, the coffee machine wheezing, gossip in every direction at full throttle, I do not know. But some do, wholly immersed in the page before them, channeling perhaps a century-old version of the Left Bank in Paris. I wouldn't under the circumstances be able to firmly commit an opening word to paper. I once was told that an admired poet, loosely of my generation, had written one of his best and later widely-anthogised poems firmly sandwiched between passengers on a long-distance flight. That's two sorts of concentration in one place. It's a valuable testament to the many and varied conditions in which writers can operate and still foster concentration. Some. The poet Schiller needed the smell of rotten apples, kept in a drawer—or was it just the core—to get him going, very pleasant and less expensive and smelly than cigarettes.

Each to her own strategy—and for each writer if she's a novelist her own room, as Virginia Woolf famously suggested, adding, with a touch of exclusivity, the necessity of having available money. Should a writer not be of independent means—I have yet to meet one who is—or a Stephen King for whom whole forests must be felled to supply the paper for his books of horror, it may be essential to regularly take the extreme measure of rising at 4 or 5 am, ahead of the family, ahead of the day job and, should there be a dedicated room, getting ahead by producing writing in it. Or follow William Faulkner's champion example when he wrote *As I Lay Dying* in six weeks after the day's wage-earning work was done and, equally, the world is dark; dedicated late-night training for the Nobel Prize. As I write this piece, in deep admiration for the foregoing necessary but not necessarily welcome strategies, the blind is partly down against a full afternoon sun, the door behind me clicked shut, while I endeavor not to squander the bright small luxury of writing they both confer and illustrate.

This in a room well-known in the household as my own, predictably so and, on this fortunate occasion so far, not an unexpected invasion of sound from without to be heard, resplendent silence in the ascendant. Knowing such fine, freakish conditions won't last, while wars flicker and flash around the planet, there are writers of literary renown who have shoved off to stay semi-permanently in remote shacks where the only sound to be heard might be the soothing rhythm of the ocean waves. Or, failing that, they've ascended the stairs in historic brick towers, located in fine rural provinces, stocked, most importantly, with books and, possibly, a secondary consideration, food and drink. There may be differing culinary imperatives depending upon whether the work at hand is a marathon, perhaps a novel, or a highly concentrated sprint, a poem. The aforementioned accommodations surpass the virtues of the stereotypical venue for a writer, the garret, not necessarily readily available. She may, even in these enlightened times of shared conjugal responsibility, have to compose her poem in her head while engaged in domestic duties, if she is to compose it at all, then commit it later to paper when the household is comatose. Or he, a traditionalist of the opposite gender, might bunk off to the garden shed in the pretense of setting in motion necessary household repairs rather than a Microsoft Word program or, for this particular guy, more likely, an old-fashioned pen. It might be cold out there. Damp.

The conditions for many, one must conclude, may not always or ever be just right to accomplish the act of writing. If the persistently annoying problem of telecommunications, for instance, can be dealt with, the writer must overcome, after a possible mild rebuke at the immediate conditions, whatever impediments to action are sure to exist and, what the hell, just get on with it, write.

Outside of libraries, where reading is expected to occur, though no longer in the formal, compulsory silence of former times, perhaps the place where one is most likely to spot a reader, possibly many, is in a waiting room. On the occasions I ever have to visit a doctor or dentist or some other professional whose focus comes complete with such a—usually generous—space, I make sure to have brought some reading material with me. Suspicion of incompetence might be attached to a specialist who can always see a client on time; a long wait equates with demand for her thorough expertise, and who wants to spend that time looking at bland furnishings, innocuous art or a sad, potted *monsteria deliciosa*. An opened book is the surest way to escape the lot. It is in waiting rooms, I've observed, where representatives of that famous class of reader, the general kind, specialists in nothing and everything, are inclined to sit, heads bowed over a book or, if foresight didn't provide one, a celebrity magazine—unless, at a fortunate stretch, there's a *National Geographic* buried under a tattered pile of *Women's Weekly*.

It is in waiting rooms where even those who might sneer at the activity of reading, read, if only the captions under the latest avalanche of photos of Brad and Angelina, no longer arm in arm, or endless other celebrities, few looking bookish. Time is the chief obvious requirement for reading, but elsewhere, more generally, away from the waiting, there may not be enough of it nowadays to save the novel, we hear from those in the trade, and there's graver news from poets. Sitting in a waiting room, where considerable and lasting opportunities for reading present themselves and, let's be optimistic, towards the future of reading, with many further opportunities to come, one and all might cheerfully conclude, as the hands move slowly around the clock on the waiting room wall, that the future of the written word in possibly any genre is, if not exactly bright, firmly assured.

On a good day, that is when it's cold, wet and dreary, the same view might be reinforced in a municipal library. Ok, most of the people visiting there are staring at computers, playing games on them, or testing their hectic attention spans on the internet. But this is a sunny fact: there will also be some steady readers and borrowers—and in the noisy kids' section, toddlers, their mothers gathered to re-inforce each other's ability to cope, who one day, should the weather favourably conspire, may well also make selections from the shelves, having heard perhaps, all over again, that the novel is dead. Or maybe he's in the poetry section, should there be one, concrete poetry suddenly the rage. Books! Books in a well-stocked library have the welcoming look of the future.

The hard, unavoidable fact—away from libraries, away from waiting rooms—is that it is cookery books that are consistently and universally read. Sell. Ignore the tedious statistics. I have tangible proof. Recently I stayed in a newly-built house, typical in size and features for its neighbourhood, and indeed others across the nation, where there were no books to be seen. No books! This for me was a disturbing experience. No matter perhaps, there was dog minding to be done, and therefore extensive walks, also newly-laid turf to be watered. The owners, a couple, relatives of my partner and, as it happens, similar in age to my children, were away on holiday. When I say no books were visible, this fact was wholly true in the living areas. In my own house, in an equivalent space, there are books shelved wall to wall, ceiling to floor. This inspires visitors, often younger than me, to ask, breathlessly 'Have you actually read all those books?' And, as if nursing some kind of shame, I quietly nod in the affirmative, adding, to be completely honest with those who are of an impressionable age, that there may be a few in the room I haven't got round to yet.

A contrasting question might be asked, by me, in the house where I recently stayed, the young couple unprepared for the potential force of it, 'Do you ever read books?' I know the answer: yes, cookery books. For tucked away in the spacious pantry of this light, airy, well-appointed, apparently books-free house, there sat an extensive row of them, hard covers and soft, jumbo and slim, a very firm indication of which books sell well among the materially well-placed young demographic the address where I was staying ably represents—of thirty-something cuisine buffs, the book buyers and readers of the future. I began peering from the street into the living areas of other fresh off-the-plan houses, while out strolling with the dog, should their curtains be parted. The result of my survey: no books. But I couldn't see into the kitchens.

Luckily I'd brought some books of my own. Books, though not of the cookery variety, are great travellers. Cookery books are poor at travel, sedentary, never go far from the stove. However I discovered on this occasion that their thematic purity was, to my considerable surprise, brazenly compromised. Tucked clandestinely between *Lotus Asian Flavours* and *Make Me a Barbecue* was a copy of a book that has been shatteringly successful, appealing, as it does, to erotic tastes—therefore aptly placed among the food porn, one might say—*Fifty Shades of Grey* its name, a sexual feast its tease. But, as I said, I was equipped with a judicious selection of my own books, a pressing need to read them and, after a cursory inspection of its style, resisted hard the temptation to read the erotic best seller.

Conditions for concentrated reading vary considerably, you may think. In the house of my young friends they were ideal, except, I need hardly to add, for the intimidating lack of books. Without the uncertain length of a wait in a waiting room, without the unpredictability of the clientele in a municipal library, the general reader may favour privacy. My friends' privacy came with two large flat screen televisions, one for each absent occupant, well-positioned enemies of the written word. They both remained dormant. The lovely nearby beach was quite possibly involved in a conspiratorial alliance with them. If to read is to diverge deeply and fruitfully from the immediate present, fact jostling with fiction, abundant silence and natural light are sympathetic companions in the matter. The new suburb of the house where I stayed is perfect for readers who haven't yet moved in. However, those proud owners who have arrived —now getting accustomed to the area and, especially, their mortgages, those life-long impediments to reading—may possibly scorn the mental elsewhere, privately enjoyed by me, and to which I ventured, between dog and lawn duties, while re-reading a Penguin Classic.

Reading, be it of fiction or about sub-atomic physics, fosters mobility while the reader sits still. It surely has a core future. Ask the folks at Kindle. Reading, for instance, on long-distance flights, on intercontinental train journeys, is parallel mobility—on any trains and boats and planes with their plentiful seating arrangements. A flight from one side of the Earth to the other, with time for sleeping, eating and maybe watching an in-flight movie or two, is about the length of an absorbing novel. This I say to comfort novices whose flying experiences thus far are squeezed in between breakfast and lunch. Only a short story or two long.

A voyage on a ship from Southampton to Sydney—it took the liner I was on over a month—is far better than a long flight. The old liner's home port in Russia may also have been fast approaching dilapidation but the small library—one of the liner's classier features—was open, impressively, at all hours, though a singular impediment to reading during the voyage across the Atlantic, through the Panama Canal, then across the Pacific, an endless voyage it seemed and therefore a marvellous opportunity for reading, was the fact that the books were written in Russian, completely foreign to me. Nevertheless, I found out, eventually, that the shipping company had been kind enough to stow in among the bulk of the books a number that had been translated into English. I plunged into them and came up with a hardback Mayakovsky. So the month-long opportunity for reading wasn't wholly squandered by playing table tennis or staring horizonwards from the corroding rails on the upper deck. Train journeys, too, are kind to the book—as non-reading passengers will observe when their eyes wander about looking for special objects of interest. In other circumstances, perhaps in towns where train journeys terminate, there may be significant impediments to the pleasurable pursuit of reading, possibly too many to mention. Or possibly not. Desire of any kind hates to be thwarted, cruelly teased. The true reader, with time available, having spotted a seat, countenances no obstacle, neither birdsong nor bustle, just gets on with it, sits down and reads.

ON SWIMMING IN THE SEA

Yesterday I anticipated writing a short piece about the sea but instead I dived into it. The sky was clear, the day windless and warm. The beach I drove to, on the bay, is a familiar one: a short, steep incline via steps to reach the sand, biscuit coloured in the bright sunlight, and from there the sea stretching to the blue horizon. It was more a necessity than a choice to go, to abandon writing about an enticing subject till, well, now. Yesterday I strode into the unusually calm water, up to my waist, and dived in. The experience was bracing. The few other people at the beach were there to sun themselves. Yesterday. Yesterday, as impossible to reclaim, except via a discernable hangover of longing, as a day four decades ago when I first discovered the beach and swam there—or indeed a day a thousand or thousands of years ago, low waves breaking, the sandstone cliffs looking on as now. Days, mostly, that merge into oblivion. Yesterday there was a freighter on the horizon. Fingerlings darted about in the warm shallows. Where I swam in the clear water—so clear and fresh that once in it you seem to immediately regain a sense of personal clarity—sunlight made restless shapes on the sandy sea floor, jazzy free-form patterns of light. On a much earlier visit, among many, I have seen a shark cruising in the water as I looked down from the cliffs. But not yesterday. Gulls, terns, cormorants, yes, both from where I stood in the water and later from where, drying off after my swim, I watched from the beach.

I am not a strong swimmer. Immersion is the thing. Though not when the sea and sand have been churned up following a storm or when there's a thorough, gloomy covering of cloud and visibility in the water is low. Then I steer clear—with daring exceptions. I want to see a shark before it sees me even though a determined shark's swimming ability is off the scale making, most likely, an advance sighting futile, fin slicing the surface of the water at some great speed as it approaches me, as on many a daring occasion I've speculated a fin might—and forget that the probability of this horror happening is, in round figures, zero.

Today, you may now have gathered, it is cloudy, the wind is up, the temperature is down —Melbourne's see-saw weather— altogether a better day to write about rather than enter the sea.

While we were chatting loosely about this briny subject recently, a friend of mine said, strikingly, you never regret taking a swim in the sea. I hastily agreed with her—it was an off-hand observation at a noisy social occasion—and I only recalled later an experience that might have checked my haste. The sea on a calm day when the sun is out always looks inviting. This is what I experienced one May bank holiday as I looked out from the foreshore, with my companion, across the English Channel. I hadn't swum at an English beach since I was a boy; now I was a man a little over forty. You can forget a lot of things during that passage of time. The day was unusually hot, the beach composed of pebbles. We took our place among the holidaymakers. Now the thing about pebble or, as they are called in England, shingle beaches is that the shingles are never the right size. If they were a few sizes larger or smaller you could comfortably walk on them barefoot. As it is, though smoothed by the motion of the tides, they are of a size that the bare, pampered human foot, used to negotiating flat surfaces in smart shoes, finds an agony to walk on. They seem to drill into the soles of the feet. To be made to run on them barefoot would be a torture suitable to yield any required confession from a tight-lipped prisoner. The best thing that can be said about them is that it's possible to find the occasional one of a suitable size, spherical, that, with a correct arm and wrist action, can be made to skim niftily, with accompanying impressive leaps, across the surface of calm sea water. This would not have been a problem on the day of our visit: there was not a single swimmer in it. As we sat, perspiring on the pebbles, this puzzled me. I put the restraint down to English reticence. There were hundreds of people roasting on the beach, the ubiquitous deckchair as ever in evidence. The water looked gorgeous. I stripped off to my togs and hobbled down towards the water, noting firmly to myself that should ever I visit such a beach again it will be with newly acquired beach footwear.

It doesn't matter whether the pebbles are above or below the waterline, they are still crippling to walk on, so when I got to the water's edge and saw that its depth fell away quickly, I wasted no time making a gingerly entrance but, spurning the pebbles, dived straight in. It seems like yesterday. The warm body adjusts to a refreshing sea temperature fairly quickly—in fifteen seconds?—and this I took for granted on that May bank holiday, freak summer weather in spring. Thirty, forty, fifty seconds later, a minute, though it seemed a lot longer, as I swam out into the English Channel, France the next landfall, I realized no adjustment was taking place. The water temperature, freezing as I probably said later, was of a kind people die quickly in. If it's possible to swerve in water, this I did, and also performed my best imitation of an exhausted cross Channel swimmer making his last strokes toward the shore where, gasping, I threw myself upon the hateful pebbles, grateful to have found them. I now knew why everybody, supine or sitting, was up on the beach. Perhaps, without exception, they were determined not to regret a sub-zero dip. Impassively looking on, they could see a man collapsed at the water's edge who bolstered their determination to remain dry. But did he, after he had at length regained his composure, regret getting wet? My friend was right. No, must be the final answer. I had rarely felt, in the water, so startlingly alive.

A contrast to yesterday's leisurely swim. But not total. We—an audacious use of the pronoun to speak for all of humanity—never regret leaping into / swimming in the sea because we emerge from the water changed, renewed and, possibly, astonished in a way no other chosen activity offers. It is possible, swimming off the coast of a Mediterranean island, to stop in shallow water and stand on a sea urchin, the pain of its barbs shooting to the cerebral cortex and then slowly abating over the course of a long fortnight—my experience but not I pray common—one's limp progressively improving, and even then not regret the swim, it being a separate matter to the blunder. The same cannot be said for swimming in a pool whether or not there's chlorine in it to sting the eyes. Pool water is tamed water, trapped. Sea water—wild, limitless—deeply refreshes, buoys the body, briskly absorbs and relieves its land bound stresses and obsessions. As such, and in such a manner earnestly expressed, immersion in the sea, if payment for entry were a requirement, could and should come with a customer guarantee—impossible, it occurs to me, for other forms of worship. Perhaps there is some deep, subconscious memory in all of us, amphibious in content, primogenitary in nature, stretching way back millions of years into deep geologic time, which attracts us to water, source of life, sea by choice, clean river or lake as consolation. Exactly as I might or might not have put it yesterday.

ON SETTLING DOWN

The comment said, 'Should do very well when he settles down.' I came across this sentence in one of my school reports while thumbing through some forgotten, recently discovered family papers. The teacher was referring to a pupil, who was nine at the time, in an all boys' school on the outskirts of Greater London. After I'd tidied the papers and placed them back in a box, that sentence is what I thought I had read. Settle down: always the hope. It resonated—continues to resonate?—decades after it had been written on the other side of the world, the boy now a man who is, shall we say, mature in years. Did his parents, dismayed by the report, instruct him to knock off the restless behaviour, quit being distracted and, in good sedentary fashion, start applying himself to his work? Probably. I forget. I returned to the box a day or so later, curious to read this and other comments again as if the ink was still assertively fresh, renew an old acquaintance, and discovered the criticism of my classroom behaviour was harsher than, in nascent kindness to myself, I'd remembered. The teacher's comment, initialled, was in fact: 'Should do very well when he calms down a little'. A nuisance kid, obviously, with something not to be calm about. I've endeavoured to teach a good number myself—kids who are resistant, unsettled at their desks, some mysterious disturbance away from the classroom directing their behaviour—and not always without success. Though it's surely possible restlessness is a personal condition for some rather than a symptom. Among the school reports I also found a circular letter sent by the headmaster to the parents of new boys at the preparatory school I was soon to attend. This would have been about two years prior to the issue of the report that now arrested my attention. Embedded in the letter was this optimistic sentence: 'I am sure he will settle down quickly'. Well, at least in one restless case, no. There are complaints aplenty in the reports about inattention and lack of concentration—and wildly varying results: top in something one year, bottom in something the next. I am sure my parents in our modest, mortgaged house, my father by day a professional man in the City of London while my mother performed her housewifely duties at home, would have adhered to the caution of their social class and thought a steady average result far better, suitably predictable in those post-war years, if only their boy would stop alarming them and settle down.

What is so intrinsically worthwhile, indeed virtuous, about settling down? What does it mean to do so? Parents, even those who've found settling down to be a domestic grind, will it on their children. They hope sooner rather than later their children will get psychologically straightened out no matter to what psychological type—the ubiquitous post-Jungian desire to categorise ever at the ready—they happen to belong. But if it's toward character—a word that's fallen from favour as a concept perhaps because it lacks contemporary psycho-medical heft—we want to give consideration, and which embraces a more capacious notion of self, (the word's origin in the Greek *charakter*, 'engraved mark', suggesting something more permanent than an attribute), I'd contend we might with benefit observe its development in tandem with the onset of bipedal activity. In other words, see the emergence of character when a child, particularly your own, suddenly has both the desire and the ability to bolt. Heraclitus wrote, 'A man's character is his fate.' This pithy, ancient philosopher knew something about change—remember? No man ever steps in the same river twice—and therefore, one may conclude, about general restlessness. As in it being a potential part of a person's character, for instance of a child easily distracted during a school lesson of no apparent interest yet riveted by others—not therefore readily prone to settling down but not immune from the prospect either. Conditional: take it or leave it.

Not long ago I received an email from a former classmate who also would have been on the receiving end of a school report written by the very teachers who'd written mine. About half a century had passed since the two of us swapped stamps and other collectables during wet weekends prior to the very unsettling decision my parents made without third-party consultation: to emigrate twelve thousand miles to Australia, rapidly executed one day on a Boeing 707. My pal from long ago, having discovered, firstly, I was temporarily living and working in London and, secondly, even more impressively, my email address, wondered in his message if I remembered him; if so, he suggested we meet. I swiftly replied in the affirmative, telling him not only did I remember him well but also his unusual middle name. I proposed a pub in Soho as the meeting place. But how will we recognise each other after all this time? I wrote, thinking of the after work crush of people. It won't be a problem, he replied.

He was right. As soon as I walked into the bar, he stepped out from the crowd to greet me. In other circumstances, without the arrangement to meet after so long, would we in utter surprise have recognised each other? We'll never have a chance to find that out. On my part, the guy who held out his hand to shake mine, who smiled broadly on seeing me in my leather coat and jeans was, in his pressed blue suit and patterned tie, most definitely and therefore recognisably a portly relative of the little guy in flannelette shorts I had known well. He'd suddenly become, my goodness, a dab hand at impersonating his possible grandfather. This meant, by extension, at a leap and bound across the decades, he was most plausibly recognisable to me as much by his appearance as by something less severely afflicted by physical change, his character. No question, it showed.

By the time we'd lavishly lubricated conversation by sinking a few pints in the hubbub of the pub, our voices rising, he seemed ever more recognisable, the same guy, the same honest stamp collector. Don't you want to know why I got in touch? he asked in his fruity Home Counties accent, after the second pint. It hadn't occurred to me there might be a specific reason. He told me he'd found, while looking through his stamp album—for the first time in decades, he reassured me as if to stress he'd generally moved on a bit—a card. He then produced it from his briefcase and asked if I recognised the picture. No, I said, I don't. Open it, he said. The writing inside, I was very surprised to find, was my own—small, compressed, from long ago. The card, with its reproduction of a Renaissance painting, was a Christmas card and in it I had written to my distant friend what I thought about unChristmassy Australian Christmasses, having by then experienced a couple, but to assure him all was well, I told him I was soon to go hunting. This was a lie. It shocked the much older me. My mother, chronically depressed after our arrival in Australia, had taken her own life, so then it was a sad family of two—my father and me—who distributed the annual Christmas cards, mostly back to the UK. Hunting! Well, what a fine thing to be tough, possibly brave and engaged in a character-building activity, as might at the time have been said. Just the thing for a wayward, restless boy. Perhaps someone had put the idea into my head, into my sights. I explained to my friend, who wished to know why reading the card had so visibly upset me, the circumstances in which it was written, the lie told. It's slipping out of his stamp album, the card I had loyally sent him, had spurred him to get in touch, to go to the trouble. Pints in hand notwithstanding, it was turning out that we were a study in contrasts, my friend's stamp album on a shelf no significant distance from where its contents were a boyhood passion, mine far away, the stamps in it, had I known when I carefully hinged them onto the pages, prophetic in their array of countries I would one day stay in or visit.

My friend had settled down quickly. He'd gone on to the public school I was once enrolled in to attend, completed a qualification, become an accountant, a profession that is still his source of income albeit unnecessary given his accumulation of wealth. His property, where the stamp album divulged its secret, is a short drive from where he grew up, I recall, in a spacious house—compared to our own—with a generous garden in a street inhabited by solid bourgeoisie. I preferred to visit him with my latest assortment of stamps rather than having him bother to visit me with his album, a car ride away. He now belonged to a gentlemen's club in the City of London, has been a member for life. If I wished to lunch with him there, which I most certainly did, foreign territory always a lure, a formal jacket and tie would be necessary. He must have guessed the wardrobe of a peripatetic ex-stamp collector would not normally yield them. Eventually, because I was wondering, he mentioned he had a wife who, he was reluctant to admit, is an alcoholic whose days are spent in her room, out of sight, like Mrs Rochester—my friend, by the way, is a champion of facts not books of fiction or any books, actually—and so, because his wife is permanently sozzled, although they live in the same house, they don't communicate. I didn't wonder aloud who drove whom around the bend or whether, more likely, it was a joint exercise. Their adult daughter, who had the good sense not to live within shouting distance of her parents, acted as an occasional intermediary. My friend, in every way well settled, except when he is following a strict itinerary as part of a classy tour group, dwells comfortably, politically on the far right. It was a United Kingdom Independence Party tie he wore to stir me up on the day we eventually met for lunch, silver wear set for four courses in his centuries-old club, two gentlemen receiving all and more-than-necessary waiter attention.

Within his life, abstracted, must lurk a possible definition of what it means to settle down for those who applaud the idea of doing so, a definition hardly necessary, the idea being central to my friend's character. Perhaps none of his school reports complained about his lack of application, his inability to settle down. Perhaps his defeated wife wishes his next package tour would morph into an endless intercontinental trek. Perhaps she reads books, has come across Bruce Chatwin's appealing idea that human restlessness persists because of the nomad, atavistically active, that exists within each of us. After all, I'd add, look at our legs, their length—haven't they evolved to handle significant perambulatory travel? To settle down or not, that may prove in an individual to be a significant conflict. By the time we'd finished our pints, the night my friend and I met in the Soho pub, and it was time to leave, we said our farewells, facing the cold night at a remarkably agreeable intersection.

ON SIGHT

If you are a dog, a Pug/Cavalier King Charles Spaniel cross, for example, since I've just returned from walking one, a powerful feature of your appreciation of the immediate world around you would involve the sense of smell. In the park, my friend's dog, like many another, is committed, while on the run, to the investigation of a spectrum of scents, his tail coiled like a spring—but which stretches out when he is relaxed—an indication of his absolute concentration. For him the park is an olfactory extravaganza. It's my guess that he visualizes what he smells; that there's more 'seeing' accomplished in the park with his flat nose than with his big eyes. Meanwhile, high above him, I'm scanning the sunny park, watching for canine threats and areas of boggy ground from yesterday's storm. It's another world up where I am, far removed from that of the dog, the laboriously evolved vantage of Homo sapiens. My own nose, comparatively redundant on this day, has little to occupy it. The council mower, initiator of the refreshing smell of cut grass, won't be turning up after yesterday's storm any time soon.

Of our five senses, six if you are adventurous, and not to belittle any of them, it's sight for the sighted which is most often dominant. We have the advantage of being able to see a long way into the distance from a bi-pedal standing position. Our range of vision, narrow compared, for example, to a frog's, is limited by the frontal position of our eyes (which is, by the way, why we're convinced adherents of watching our own backs—where the sixth sense may really kick in) but our horizons are far. I am making this standard point to get to another. What we see in the light of an average day or starry night is not sufficient to satisfy us.

We simply want to see a lot more; our eyes are not up to the job. I am not talking about going to the absurd lengths of climbing the world's highest mountain to get a better view of the local topography or, for that matter, voyaging into space to get a better take on the spherical shape of the planet we tenuously inhabit. Or, in prospect for those so inclined in our fallen world, of seeing the

Lord our Maker, the veil on limited earthly vision miraculously lifted—seeing not smelling Him, please note, the sense of sight one must presume all-conquering in the hereafter. No, forget these. Vision of some kind has likely been around in creatures on Earth for some half a billion years—now that's surely memorable—since the evolutionary event known as the Cambrian explosion. That's a lot of days and nights for the sense of sight to get perfected—a matter championed by the philosopher William Paley who viewed the eye as evidence of Godly design. (Aside: some years ago, out of necessity, I visited an eye specialist with a very promising name, Dr Wise who, although married to a philosopher, had never heard of the Argument from Design which, to me, patient placing trust in the specialist, was not at all promising.) Yes, the eye is a fine organ but, in spite of the theological and evolutionary encomiums recommending it, limited in scope. As I tentatively prepare for a forthcoming trip, set off to see another part of the world, this has become freshly, optically clear.

That we generally see things in relation to ourselves is a given: that's a big, embarrassing spot on my nose, that's a big, ugly building in front of me, that's a stunningly big mountain I don't want to climb. Big has shifting, subjective occasions, ditto for those that are little. Eventually, however, the naked eye will significantly let us down. It is equipment that comes to the necessary rescue: electron microscopes to probe the mysteries of the sub-atomic world, powerful telescopes in remote locations to explore the reaches of the unfathomable universe. Our collective view of things, large or small, is dimmer without them. Unless, like that visionary William Blake, you can see a world in a grain of sand—though it's perfect proof for the literalist that appearances can be deceptive. A notion I have temporarily rejected, fast as swivelling my head, and in its place substituted seeing is believing as an opposing, useful replacement truth underpinned, I should state, by the aid of minor optical equipment, for clearly, soon, in some other clime, it is the sense of sight which will be my dominant guide. Aristotle, who regarded seeing as being the superior sense, would approve. There are two, only two, items already anxiously placed in my small suitcase: a pair of goggles for subaqueous exploration and a pair of binoculars to scan obdurate land—equipment, now out of sight but not possibly overlooked at the last minute before departure, to view very soon, deeply and widely, other locations.

ON GETTING THE UNEXPECTED

The earthquake happened two hours after we arrived. The bus, packed with locals, mostly large elderly women in sombre clothes with shopping beside them, had driven us from Mytilene, the largest town, a port, here on Lesbos. It was mostly a slow journey and could not be otherwise. The narrow road winds through mountainous country, olive trees growing behind drystone terraces wherever possible, descends into a ravine, then stays close to a stream, still flowing, even though the heat of summer has arrived, which provides for a corridor of lush vegetation, including bright oleanders and plane trees. When the bus reaches a severe, blind bend, the driver toots his horn. His hand is never far from tooting it though fortunately there is not much traffic on this road. Along the way, the bus stops at small villages, dropping off passengers who farewell family or friends still to arrive at their destinations. Those who stay on the bus until its final destination will have been travelling, often next to a sheer incline, for an hour and a half. The road is not one for an inexperienced bus driver. Or, for that matter, any other novice driver.

The bus terminates at about the same time each day in the main *plateia* of the coastal town of Plomari. This is where we have come to spend much of the summer. It's a fine town, we decided on a visit some time ago; above the *plateia*, houses, many built over a century ago—and there are older stone buildings as well—are positioned on a steep slope overlooking the harbour. There are views across the Aegean Sea to the neighbouring island of Chios and to mountainous Turkey, both at this time of year often in a vaporous heat-haze. Apart from olives—there are roughly eleven million olive trees on Lesbos—we discovered that Plomari produces what is reputed to be the best ouzo in Greece. It also harbours numerous wooden one and two man fishing boats that look exceptionally small and vulnerable when, seen from a high vantage point, they are heading out to sea for long hours, often for the night, until they return heroically the following morning. Another aspect of the local economy is, of course, tourism but not to the all-encompassing degree that it is on some other Greek islands where there is no avoiding the change it has wrought, olive groves a backdrop to boozy Greek theme parks. So let me gently propose that it is a discerning tourist — who, with sufficient time earned elsewhere at his or her disposal, might actually prefer to be called, more seriously, a traveller, interested in the history and culture and perhaps even geology of a destination, rather than, soon enough, simply its bars—who'd choose Plomari as a place to prop.

Our specific address, pre-arranged, is particularly attractive to us because of its elevation, high above the coastal road, the nearest *taverna*, and a small church with its blue dome and white cross. There was no time to lose after our arrival: we had been living out of travel bags for weeks and now, at last, we could unpack. Our landlady from, we gathered, a well-established old family in Plomari, was perhaps already identifying us to her kin as the couple from Australia, visible, both him and her, as fair-skinned beneath their wide-brimmed hats. We distributed some of our belongings about the rented premises, congratulated ourselves on the choice, made a late, light lunch, and then, since wi-fi is available, checked for messages and news from afar on our digital devices. Evidence that, in the second decade of the third millennium Common Era, we were well advanced in making ourselves right at home here in relatively slow, remote to us Plomari—to the point where one of us, so relaxed, had put his feet up—when the earthquake struck.

The shaking was violent, protracted and extremely alarming—as was the noise of it, a deep grating and rumbling sound, like an omnipresent form of slow-motion collision. Without having had any prior experience of such an event, I knew this was indisputably an earthquake. The white room I was in shook. The two of us, the strangers from afar, and now from separate rooms were, with no time to lose, both at the front door in unison and then rapidly out of it. To be alarmed is not to be scared, which might be debilitating, one's faculties frozen as, proverbially, the hair on one's head. Alarm makes for action. We were not alone out on the street cut high into the rocky incline; others' instant reaction was also to flee the wobbling buildings, each with its splendid view, each now seemingly on a precarious perch. By the time the violent shaking and deep rumbling had ceased—a matter of seconds that were nevertheless in our minds remarkably stretched—the event (but was this just the first indication of something truly calamitous?) showed how swiftly a crisis propels people into a state of sudden unity. And with very specific application to this wholly unexpected situation, propel them, suddenly wide-awake, out of the Greek version of an afternoon siesta. The disturbance immediately replaced, in the startling silence, by the sound of men, women and children talking out in the street as if quietly swapping opinions about a theatrical event from which they had all just emerged. Close-knit, neighbourly, and a very impressive human response to shock. We, the strangers in their company, didn't let ourselves down with rival behaviour. However, feelings later would shift.

The news media, which in all circumstances never have time to lose, swiftly reported that the quake had registered 6.4 on the Richter scale, occurred at 3.28pm and had its epicentre in the Aegean Sea eleven kilometres south of Plomari. That is a position we could guess at spotting from our balcony. From there, after with re-established dignity we'd returned through the front door, I could see that a cross and its base had toppled from the church tower on the road below and lay as rubble. A few books I'd unpacked and placed on a shelf only an hour or so earlier were now on the floor. In the bathroom, some toiletries had eagerly sought it too. With unwitting foresight, I had yet to unpack my aids to visual reconnaissance: a pair of binoculars (terrestrial use) and a set of goggles (submarine use). Both useless in the event of an earthquake. For I can now testify, one earthquake being indisputably representative of all others, that they are everywhere to be felt and nowhere to be seen—like, some would say, God. In the case of the earthquake that we, newly arrived, took as our own, it had no precedent. Neither, most obviously, during the two hours we had been in the region nor, we soon learned, in the living memories of its ancient citizens with wizened faces who had spent their lives in it. This being the case, since memorable seismic events are largely beyond human prediction, our timing to experience one was impeccable.

Today we have the science of plate tectonics to account for the rubble I've seen down the road and seismographs to record the force that caused it. However, were the finger to be pointed at Poseidon, the god of the sea in Greek mythology, or some other troublesome deity in ancient times, there's not much to separate the touted efficacy of scientific knowledge from the hidden logic of the gods in terms of knowing where and when both citizenry and their shelter will next be shaken. Images of the collapsed stone houses in a village five kilometres from here are quickly there for all to see on the internet. One of the villagers, a forty-five year old woman, is dead; the injured are said to number about ten. To the west of here, because of a landslide, the coast road is closed. Close by, there are old houses with new cracks; fallen pediments that smashed on impact. We receive emails from home expressing concern. Our landlady, a strong woman with solid views, apologises for the scare, hoping no doubt we won't flee. Apologises for whom? The township? Nobody thinks straight after absorbing an earthquake. The damage is unevenly distributed. It's a shift, seven kilometres deep, in a tributary of the jagged Great Anatolian Fault (with which the inhabitants of Istanbul have long been intimately acquainted) that is to blame, I discover, in a state of later composure. So that is the culprit but it seems natural to wonder, obsessively, post-quake, when and with what force is it likely to be so again?

The first aftershock is almost as unnerving as the earthquake itself. Is it a sign of stronger or weaker shocks to come? An earthquake superseded soon afterward by a more powerful one is relegated by seismologists to a less esteemed category and called a foreshock. Time will tell where we have stood, unsettled, in the unfolding chain of seismic events. When inside the house, we leave the front door open. The initial aftershock, its low rumble, so soon an unnecessary reminder of what had come before, spurred us to make for the front door once again. It's no wonder many of the townsfolk, we later find—a few aftershocks later—gathered in the *plateia*, have apparently determined to sleep outside, away from the buildings that no longer look to be so certain of remaining upright. However, I reason, at a time when being reasonable may not count for anything much, there is probably as much chance of another major quake happening in the next few starlit hours as there is sometime next week, next month, next year or in the next fifty. No expert can know. Getting the night right to sleep outside will be a matter of potluck. What is a matter of certainty is that there are sure to be future aftershocks to, one hopes, unimpressively test the town's foundations, a town in which, it eventually transpired, the greater majority of houses are officially declared safe. Others, bereft of some masonry, are cordoned off, cordons soon to be ignored as regular life here in Plomari, in its modest shops and cafes and houses, begins to resume, Greek fatalism kicking in.

So we chose not to join the rough sleepers, one of us on the receiving end of some mild coercion from the other, and fitfully slept inside, not disappointed by a lack of aftershocks of varying strength. It was like being on a slow overnight train, all smooth going, which suddenly judders at intervals to a halt. But in the case of this particular experience, after the juddering, sleep does not come so easily. I forget how many times we sprang in alarm from the bed to make for the front door. There was no need to start awake, relieved, from some unsettling dream; waking reality, in the dead of night, had it all. I had every expectation of never forgetting it. Ever since I was a boy, growing up in seismically boring countries, I've been fascinated by geomorphology, alerted to it early on by the knowledge that the Earth as we see it today wasn't made by a divine power in seven days—though I knew parts of old Genesis by heart—but over billions of years, and is still unfinished business. I knew that, somewhere beyond my experience, the Earth's surface moves. Now, after a significant passage of personal time, this was within my experience. Feelings about some experiences, one repeatedly learns, may be mixed. The repetition of aftershocks drums this in—a frontline lesson never to forget within a significant aspect of geomorphology, the Earth's crust reminding us during the night that it buckles.

It gives cliffs, of which there are many here, natural along the coast, manmade when appearing as cuttings for roads, a newly arresting quality. Not in relation to composition, of course, often

39

schist in this part of the island, but in relation to the cliffs' permanence. Up close, and it's difficult not be close to them, sheerness being a defining feature of the place, this is a pressing concern. The schist together with the accompanying varieties of sedimentary rock are often crumbly. Looking at them directly from below seems, in this obviously unstable place, to be tempting something. This feeling still has undiminished currency, now that a week has passed, since our major seismic experience.

When something dramatically unexpected like this happens, and who in sensible comfort would wish to recount the many forms of alarm they've experienced in a lifetime, threat may begin to seem to be at large and looming beyond its recent specific preserve. I am not alone in being wary of any number of nearby cliffs. Tourists, with their much-needed money, are no longer coming in predicted numbers—there had been a recovery since the influx of refugee arrivals by boat, during the Syrian civil war, had declined—but a politician, promising nothing beyond the comfort of his presence, does front up. The old men, as if nothing would shift them, go on sitting outside the cafes, rituals fixed. Yet the undamaged school, in a state of bureaucratic paralysis, has not re-opened. Each day, by mid-afternoon, the onshore breeze regains it authority. Down the road, the rubble from the cross that fell from the church tower is gone. I walk past the church, in the early mornings, to buy fish from the boats newly returned to the harbour. The morning sunlight makes the calm sea look burnished. The houses on the hillside seem like immemorial witnesses to the comings and goings of the freshly painted fishing boats. It's a beautiful place. I swim each day. Aftershocks, now fewer in number and lower in magnitude, continue. The cliffs hold steady. For my rock collection, far away, I find samples, schist a must. We greet at the beach our new friend who owns the nearest *taverna*. The ouzo is good. From our balcony, we spot passing dolphins, grab the binoculars. We have no plans for soon moving on. Through olive groves, up a steep stone path, an ancient access, we climb until there's a fine view of Plomari, the town in which we were severely shaken. On the surface, for all now to see, it might never have happened.

ON THE HALLELUJAH AND OTHER SHADOWS

A love of shadow must imply a love of the sun. They are complementary. However, who during the summer months in Greece would want, when the sun is high in the sky, to walk or sit or lie in its direct rays? The heat of that star will melt bitumen, the reason why, I suppose, the steep road we climb home is made of thick, ridged concrete. It is certainly why I wear a hat with a brim, provider of mobile shade. Shadow is shade when, with relief, you are standing in it. No sensible Greek would choose to do otherwise. Ask one a question or engage in conversation out in the heat of the day and he or she will quickly guide you into the nearest convenient shade from a tree or a building until the talking is done. It is unthinkable to stand in the sun. The sunlight on the sea or on the terracotta roofs of the houses is a fine thing to look at but best appreciated from the shade. Big, red, fully ripened tomatoes are picked by their grower in his domestic plot, where zucchinis and melons and cucumbers and beans also grow in abundance, but only when the angle of the sun's rays are oblique, the shadows, the admirable shadows, by then gaining in length.

May and June have passed, since we have been here on the island of Lesbos, and now it is well into July, the hottest month of the year. It is only the visitors from northern Europe who, in their swimwear, lie in the sun. There is a lot of vitamin D storage going on—replenishment after the passing of the dreary, dark months those northern bodies have endured in heavy clothes. It's concerning for us to witness these people lying for hours on the beach, as we walk along the road in shadow from a cliff, out of their sun-blinded sight. Don't they know about the dangers? The shadowy couple—us—from Australia certainly do. The value of shade for vulnerable skin has become a drummed-in national assumption. Who'd rebel for the hell of it now? That is why those northerners won't see us lying flat out on the beach in the midday sun, as if we're concussed, after taking a dip in the sea. Nor will a sane Greek. Not, at any rate, here. Perhaps at resorts where everyone's folly is also on holiday.

Fishermen, should they set out by day from the nearby harbour in their small boats, unfold shades on permanent frames. The stray cats and dogs, of which there are many, claim shade where providence delivers it: a doorstep perhaps or a bench. If it is afternoon and therefore very hot, a lot of good shade is occupied. Shade not shadow; shadows are for foreign eyes now seeking the picturesque. All around the town's *plateia*, while businesses are closed for the afternoon, those folk sitting at the older cafes and along narrow side streets, where the air finding a passage is coolest and the shade deepest, settle, just this side of sleep, on the quotidian. It does not require sunglasses.

The playful name I have given to a particular shadow I like a lot has, in our household, stuck: it is the Hallelujah Shadow. I cannot praise it enough. Daily. There are shadows that may cancel out the light from a life; there are shadows of disaster. The world of metaphor has many shadows in it. They do not generally bring joy. The Hallelujah Shadow does. From where I'm positioned on our balcony in the early evening, it is without peer. E M Forster said 'we cast a shadow on something wherever we stand'. I get what he means. I'm in a sitting position when from the balcony, high up on an incline, I slowly take in the 180° views. To the south, across the Aegean Sea, the coasts of both Turkey and the Greek island of Chios are visible. This is where in recent years some refugees cross, though not lately. To the west, there's a bluff into which the coast road has been cut. To the east, a view of Plomari town and its harbour, walking distance along the coast road, although a walk along it after the sun has established itself in the sky until it sets provides testimony to the body's useful ability to react to extreme daytime heat by luxuriously drenching itself in perspiration. There is no shade from trees along the road. The Hallelujah Shadow eventually takes this route.

This shadow is reliable in a country where reliability is often a stranger in human affairs. Who'd want to turn up to fix a tap or countersign a contract when it's 40° centigrade out on the street? What taxi driver wouldn't want to have a smoke in the shade of a tree? Or sleep? By the time I'm out on the balcony, freshly showered in cold water after the excesses of personal leisure activity, reading for instance, the fierce rays of the sun strike the town and its harbour at a relatively low angle, although the temperature hasn't budged much since noon, unless it's gone further up. I've poured myself a drink, two if I'm to be joined in the celebration. The shadow begins slowly to lengthen at first, from where I observe it, across a terracotta roof obliquely below. By now, the swallows are about, dozens that swoop, glide and soar, their squeals thin and piercing. It's the hour for small flying insects. The swallows fly close to me; our balcony is sufficiently high up. The sun is lowering in the west and the shadow is proceeding dutifully towards the east. It's getting away from me but this, remember, is an occasion for celebration. Over several more rooftops it goes, improving its extent, until I, distracted by the squealing birds or nets laid at impressive length from a fishing boat out at sea or by some internal domestic business, then notice the shadow has reached the cliffs next to the coast road and is advancing toward the bleached distance. The shadow now has impressive width and depth and gets the better of every feature it meets; soon much of the coast road itself with its toy-like parked cars. What I am watching is the triumph of shadow over light; it is epic. This particular shadow, as the westering sun declines to the height of the bluff and the ridge proceeding inland from it—hidden from my view—is a giant among shadows. It is now approaching the town and soon will cool the harbour wall where, at its elbow, there are tables, chairs and a family *kafeneio* to serve those in the evening who will occupy them, perhaps us. I can see, without my binoculars, its lights go on when the Hallelujah Shadow reaches it. They intensify as the light continues to fade. The air cools. Now, as the earth continues to revolve on its axis, it is time for the assertion of that global lasting shadow, vast and deep under the stars, which frees the town's children from their parents and the confinement of houses to go out and play—to scoot, run and shout along the actively sociable streets. Permitted equally—in binary agreement—by the sun.

ON BOTHERING TO TRAVEL

The man knew everything necessary and I knew little or nothing. That's how I saw it then, that's how I see it now—now that he's far away, though only recently so. Travel, for all of its pleasures, revelations and personal tests, is a questionable pursuit when you, the experienced traveller, turn up in a foreign place the locals rarely, if ever, leave. Who is the wiser? Or as the poet Elizabeth Bishop asked, 'Is it lack of imagination that makes us come/ to imagined places, not just to stay at home?' A mere square metre of earth, in any specified country, may be replete with micro-organisms, minerals and mysteries, enough to keep a scientist or anyone, of the right inclination and with the right specialist equipment, at home in stationary contemplation for an age, a lifetime, with no desire to budge. During one of those long occasions in a doctor's waiting room, I read, as anyone would who has a taste for travel while stalled for an indeterminate time, a feature article about Prince Edward Island in a *National Geographic* magazine. At some point, during its exploration of the geography, history and economy of the place, an elderly man, asked how he viewed his Canadian province, was quoted as saying, 'It's the best place in the world'. This spurred the writer to expose, with metropolitan relish, the old guy as a true Prince Edward Islander by asking him where else he has seen. 'Nowhere else', he proudly replied. Lucky man, I thought, restlessness getting the better of me among the forlorn, seated patients. I was among them to have a cyst on my back treated; it might have been better and more swiftly accomplished on wonderful Prince Edward Island. From a confirmed and unwavering perspective, a place never to want to leave—and, who would care to doubt it, a wise thing for a contented man to believe. When, in the 1930s, the then neglected Australian painter, Clarice Beckett was asked by a colleague if she planned, as was fashionable for artists, to travel to far away Paris, her reply was firmly negative. She had questioned the need to travel and found it wanting when, as she explained—and I'm paraphrasing—after many years of painting *en plein* air on the cliffs

45

and beaches of the bayside suburb where she lived, she far from found it wanting. In fact, in a state of continuous and still unsatisfied discovery, the area was her utterly absorbing subject and Paris the equivalent, in comparison, of a paltry postcard view dropped into a letterbox. Evidence of a failure, perhaps, of its sender's imagination.

However, I knew nothing, beyond what I could deduce and imagine, about the man who knew everything necessary. He had a great deal to say. But I understood not a word. There was no introducing ourselves, no exchanging of names. Besides, meteorological matters were happening fast. The man's face was severely weathered, leathery and lined. We came to share our situation in this way. That day I had visited, in good company, a small town close to the coast called Behramkale in the Turkish province of Çanakkale. Our travels by good fortune, on the day in question via an unexpected lift in car, had taken us there. Also known as Assos, especially to students and experts in classical history, it's a destination for the reasonably fit. For the unfit or those passing through, its acropolis will remain an impressive prominent feature in the distance. A student or expert in geology will tell you that it is located on a trachyte crag—a new feature to me—igneous rock, of which it is a type, dominating the area. We climbed the crag, past old stone houses, up steep basaltic flagstone streets. Aristotle founded an academy in about 350 BC and married there. St Paul, with altogether another nascent calling, visited in the first century AD. He would have seen, on the summit, perhaps with detached, self-permitting aesthetic pleasure, the Temple of Athena. We walked about, in the considerable heat of the day, what was left of it.

I realized for the first time that I'm over being readily awed by ancient ruins unless they come up with something markedly unexpected. How many towering Doric columns, wandered around, does it take to reach this critical point? There's no accurate counting. At Assos, I can confidently report, only six remain. Travel has its casualties. Most impressive was the view from the temple across the Aegean Sea, changing dramatically in the changing light, the Greek island of Lesbos anchored on the horizon. An approaching storm had swept the light from it. We had, days earlier, arrived from Lesbos by boat, the sea calm, dolphins breaking surface. Now any such passage would already be turbulent. The predominance of white caps way out at sea made this apparent even though the storm front had yet to reach us. Lightning, distant, forked and flickered against the dark veils, hanging from the ominous summer storm clouds, which were sign of torrential rain. There were few people within the boundary of the temple to witness this, to be worried about the stumbling, approaching heavy thunder. I knew foreign visitor numbers to Turkey had collapsed in the wake of recent terrorist attacks, highly visible, and because of the incumbent Turkish president's autocratic abuses of human rights, not so visible. I couldn't see either of these seriously alarming matters—should we submit to terrorists and stay away, boycott the whole country because of one power-mad, paranoid man?—being of immediate, necessary concern to the small numbers of Turkish daytrippers who were strolling about. The concerns of the keen contemporary traveller on this far-from-home foreign soil, represented by the two of us, obtain a different perspective in the local for whom accessibility to sites is relatively easy—still a right!—and safely close to home. Well, that's my perspective now that I've left. Besides, the thing that visibly concerned them, us, everyone together, more than the plight of the country as a whole, was that the wind was getting up, then came the rain, and soon all of the ingredients of an awe-inspiring, gods-at-war electrical storm. The ruined Temple of Athena was no place for a mortal to be.

The man who knew everything who, by chance, I'd encounter a couple of hours later as a result of our hastened departure from Behramkale, had probably never climbed the trachyte crag—where now up the road are stalls and cafes and gypsy women selling, for a song, handmade wooden spoons—to make a specific visit to the Temple of Athena. Surely, he'd have better, necessary things to do as, later, I would readily conclude. But right then the storm was happening, shelter necessary, though not for long—the storm was as quickly upon us as it was gone. We were staying many miles away, near the coast, and now left wondering how to return. Behrankale could boast a single ATM but not a single taxi. Nor, it seemed, running buses. The people spoke a dialect of Turkish that might have eloquently told us many things we wanted to know about transportation if we could have understood the language; however during any possible response to an unintelligible question about the matter, we might as well have had plugs in our ears. It's in this kind of unbidden situation where the experience of travel reaches a pitch of intensity—as if while standing at an unfamiliar crossroads without signposts one's life depended on guessing the single necessary direction for escape—that the element of chance comes in. There was no ruined Temple of Fortuna in which to pray for good luck. Chance: it's what, in retrospect, gives independent travel its edge, its arresting uncertainties. The exposure to these coupled with the preternatural paying of attention to one's surroundings. Along with the transport problem, we also hadn't foreseen that the day would cool so quickly; dressed lightly for the heat, we were tested by the unexpected. So what to do next?

Gypsy women tell fortunes. The one who suddenly assailed me on the street—close, as it happened to a sad, empty little bus shelter—delivered an indecipherable sales pitch for, presumably, wooden spoons. We, on that late afternoon of pressing imperatives, required no more than the several we'd already purchased and had about us enough to be considered an over supply of them. The elderly gypsy in her drab, once colourful clothes, was obviously very poor; but she was my kind of stereotype. Detained on the deserted street, happy to pay, how could I implore her to tell me my fortune? Would things start looking up? In the midst of hopeless negotiations of sorts, possibly still about spoons, she became good fortune's agent. A little bus, a *dolmus*, pulled up, out of nowhere it seemed, next to the non-descript bus shelter. Unseen by me, my companion had waved it down. My detainment by the gypsy was luck in disguise. Before due thanks and appreciation could be uttered and not understood, the *dolmus* was gone, going in the desired direction, two foreigners now comfortably on it.

Çannakkale province is in northwestern Turkey and coastal. It has very hot summers. It feels exposed. The storm we'd experienced was unusual at that time of year, more so the second front still to come. The bus travelled through open, basaltic, sparsely populated country where hardy vegetation is low to the ground. It is undulating land, craggy and parched. Sheep country, stone sheepfolds a feature, and tough there to be a sheep. Or, occasionally, beside the road, an enduring goat. The bus driver responded to requests to set passengers down and pick others up, country people in durable well-worn clothes. It was a slow journey; along the long and meandering road there was little traffic. Our destination was many miles off it but, sure enough, the bus would pass our turn off to Kuruoba, the village a side road passes through on the way to the coast and the place where we were staying. There would be some walking to do, the day so much cooler, stratocumulus clouds by now allowing the appearance of patchy sunlight.

It was while I was watching the little bus after it had stopped for us to alight, departing on its tireless way into the distance, I noticed, to the north, the sky again was darkening. At the turn off stood in stark isolation a concrete bus shelter: four walls, a doorway (no door), and four windows (unglazed). It was dark in there and bare. I am keeping my companion mostly out of this account not wishing to hazard assumptions about her raw subjective experience. The veracity of the telling and the emphases are, perhaps recklessly, mine alone. However at this point I can say with confidence that we soon both shared a pressing dilemma: should we leave the bus shelter behind and strike out on foot for the coast and our accommodation, an hour or more away, or take a shine to the shelter as a minimalist architectural triumph and stay close to or in it? Another huge storm front was fast approaching. The frequency of its forked lightning, striking the earth with fabulously random abandon, would make any cheap temptation to reach for hyperbole unnecessary. I confess: the lightning was frightening. Our decision: there was only one place to be.

The rain, when it arrived, dashed by the wind, came plentifully into the shelter and, roughly coinciding with this a man of the land stepped in, rough clothes, brown weathered face. He had left his bicycle next to the step. Now, I saw that placing a lightning conductor so close to the bus shelter as being a foolish act, as in fact being at the extremity of foolishness, but even if he could have heard me express this while the terrible thunder shook the earth and our shelter, it would have been useless: this Turk could understand not a word that I said nor I his many lengthy assertions. I reckoned on him being a shepherd and shepherds being all-knowing about the elements, it was clear now that he too, a man of this rugged open country, had taken shelter to wait out the storm, and that we'd managed to crib some basic wisdom from somewhere by choosing to do so as well. He studied me with the alert eyes of a wild animal, quick, shifting about, scanning me up and down to fathom me—and as he did so he spoke with a remarkable fervor, all the more so for the startling gibberish he heard come out of my mouth. It made him laugh. Surely, this was his first verbal encounter with a foreigner, fair-skinned, an idiot. I could see the crazed verticals of lightning striking around us through a window. The man who, with his back to it, knew everything necessary, if only he could get it across, had a way of standing very close to me, an opposing conception of personal space, emphasizing each of his points by jabbing his forefinger at me as if in so doing I might eventually, sudden as a thunderclap, come to my senses and comprehend him. All I knew right then was that I was out of my depth in a wet bus shelter; a man, with his companion, poorly dressed for the weather, who has travelled far and with much prior experience of doing so, now in the company of another man, suitably garbed, who can see, most obviously and correctly, which of the two of us is the better equipped on the day for human existence and, with a further assertive display of his finger, sufficiently at home in the local, the familiar, the deeply known. Which summons another point, exactly, why from it ever bother to go?

ON BEING SINCERE

This morning I walked near a park bench, as I frequently do, on which there's a small metal plaque. It reads—

Henry Joseph Kata
8 April 1951 – 2 September 2012

It all began here with soft rain falling.
My soulmate and love, you are so missed.

When I am in the vicinity of the bench—it's in a quiet, shady spot—here in inner-Melbourne, I'm on my way to the supermarket. The first time I noticed the plaque and then stopped to read it—a few months ago, about four years after the death of Henry Joseph Kata—I was so moved by its simple eloquence, sincerity and the import of the loss on the person whose words they are, that I suddenly entered into a kind of sympathetic mourning and hung around for some time out of respect. The bench may not have been there for long, council approvals being notoriously slow, and since the route I take to the supermarket is relatively new to me, I can't say when the bench was first put in place. I'd go for recently. I'd guess there was a quiet ceremony, in attendance the deceased's companion and those closest to, I am assuming, her. Attached to the slats of the bench, next to the plaque, there is always a sprig of fresh rosemary. The soulmate's bereaved returns often, possibly daily and, I expect, sits on the bench with her memories. Communes. Although the bench is for public use in a public space, a bench among other benches placed around the large, leafy park in positions where shade or a broad view is maximized, I would feel as if I was invading another's intimate space if ever I sat on it. So I don't. Maybe, one day, grocery bag in hand, I'll see from a distance Henry Joseph Kata's soulmate attaching a fresh sprig of rosemary or quietly sitting out the afternoon, alone.

*

51

A bench with a memorial plaque I have sat on is in Soho, London. I deliberately did so, made a point of it. The plaque reads—

Kirsty MacColl 1959–2000

One day I'll be waiting there
An empty bench in Soho Square

The words, adjusted from second to first person, are MacColl's own, taken from one of her most loved songs. A speedboat hit and killed her instantly in a swimmers and divers only area off the coast of Mexico. The driver of the boat, owned by a tycoon, was never charged. MacColl, as her core fans will attest, was one of the finest singer-songwriters around: when her melodies aren't hauntingly lovely, they're cheerfully uptempo, sometimes with a Latin-American flourish, and her lyrics, sharp enough to cut, often witty, are the product of a quick intelligence. It is often the music of someone defiantly trying to beat the odds. Her hardline socialist, singer-songwriter father, Ewan MacColl—he wrote 'Whenever I saw her face' a huge hit for Roberta Flack—left her mother, Jean, when his daughter was a baby. Kirsty MacColl's marriage to a record producer, which produced two children, didn't last. Stage-fright paralysed her. Her records, praised in the music press—though this didn't translate into big sales—failed to make her, even remotely, a household name. Diving off the coast of Mexico, she didn't notice in time a speedboat fast approaching, her looming fate.

When the fatal accident happened, things were looking up for MacColl both musically—a lavishly praised new CD—and emotionally, which compounded the shock for family, friends and fans. Her oeuvre suddenly seemed even more poignant. While I didn't think it appropriate to sit on the bench in the inner-Melbourne park, the one in Soho Square was a different prospect. I had a sincere desire to do so and wasn't put off, on the day I first went to inspect it, by the fact that others had got there before me and, judging by their easy youth, surely had never heard of Kirsty MacColl. Those who loved her had raised funds for the bench, got the necessary authorities on side, had it placed between others near the south entrance gate, and organized a well-attended unveiling ceremony. This is a public bench in a public space where those who go in homage from near and far, anonymously, are, so those who placed the bench hope, over the years, an ever-growing busy intersection of admirers. I took my own turn to sit, recall a haunting song, and contemplate the Square that inspired it.

*

It is surely a strange thing to have definite feelings for someone you do or did not know, will never meet—intimate sincere feelings which will never get roughed up by personal contact. Perhaps it's easiest to be sincere about someone who isn't physically around; a good reason, surely, why some people pray. The communication, handily, is all one way, untroubled by oppositional static: an outpouring of words from—whom? It doesn't matter; what does is that it happens. It helps, though it's not essential, for there to be a physical object to provide a tangible focus for one's feelings: a religious effigy, a secular plaque, a bench in the park. Conduits to those who were once with us, now departed, though clearly not without trace, the hardly deceased.

*

Sincerity, there's a lot of it about after a death—some of it sincere. Each memorial park bench—common now that the erection of marble in graveyards is in steep decline, cremation for as long as I can remember in the rapid ascendant—attests to tested sincerities. I once knew a woman, stayed in her house, who deviated, failed the sincerity test, collected sums of money to pay for a bench—great position stated, views, veritable real estate—to commemorate the life of the man whom she claimed was her soulmate. However since a decade had passed since his death, time enough even for a local council to flick the light to green, it was apparent she'd diverted the contributions into more pressing uses, such as a trip to L.A. No sprig of rosemary required for the commemorative bench, no chance passer-by to notice it.

*

Three decades after my mother died, my father received a letter from the crematorium where in 1962 a rose had been planted in her memory, a simple plaque installed at the foot of the bush, facing a path, and accomplished without delay. A red rose in a long row of many, many intersecting rows: a challenge to locate, a challenge rarely taken. The formal letter with its, ahem, 'Yours sincerely' valediction kindly requested to know whether he would like to extend the existence of the memorial plot, a significant four figure sum of money the fee, for a further term. Otherwise, for the rose, for the memorial plaque, things were terminal in the crematorium. The first correspondence he'd had in thirty years concerning his 'loved one' from that thriving, voracious, ever-expanding Melbourne business, it came as a shock. The memorials weren't there in perpetuity? Most certainly not. My father swiftly called a meeting; I arrived on time. The minutes, had they been written down, would record a unanimous decision that permitted the crematorium to uproot the rose, remove the plaque, and in so doing, at least in regard to this particular temporal matter, no further correspondence would be necessary. We had decided that acting now was no worse, indeed better, than troubling a later generation of the family to face up to this lucrative con and act. Besides, and this I suppose made it easy, it was in the first place standard and slick good form to lease a plot (and forget, if ever my father was told, it was merely leased) for a rose and a plaque—wasn't there evidence aplenty that bereaved consumers thereabouts did much the same, rosebuds abounding beyond counting?—and then be as correspondingly quick, with a signature, to hurry it most sincerely into oblivion.

ON LOOKING INTO MIRRORS

You look into the mirror. There are a number about the house and every now and then one of them becomes an attraction. Your skin is clear. Your hair is thick. The face looking back at you is as it should be when you are about to leave the house. A bit serious, perhaps. You think, while somehow entranced by the enigma of yourself in reverse image, that you'd better get a move on—but you don't think, in this the twentieth year of your life, goodness, don't I look young. That's one thing, in front of a mirror, you have never thought and, personal history suggests, vanity notwithstanding, won't ever.

Time passes. A lot of time—though relatively little, in fact an inconsequential amount of time for the earth, upon which you dwell, as it journeys eternally around the sun—but it's a great deal of time for you, now getting ready to go out. You look into the mirror. It is a mistake to do this. There are several mirrors in the house, several too many; a couple more than there are members of the household. Your skin has wrinkled. Your hair has thinned. This has happened without due consultation with the enigmatic person who stares back at you. It is an outrage. You look like one of those marginal people who it was not within your comprehension ever to be: a grandparent. So why don't you feel like one? This development seems to have been rather sudden. Each time you are surprised to find yourself in the unkind mirror, you most certainly do think, accurately, in this, the sixty-something year of your life, goodness, don't I look old. That's one thing, you ruthlessly admit, you will continue to do.

*

I employ the generic 'you' incautiously. I have not methodically gathered evidence for the foregoing 'universal' state of affairs. There may be members of the generation to which I belong who by a freak of nature or having discovered the elixir of youth—a compound found, so I've read, in avocadoes, cucumbers and

55

broccoli, favourite foods of mine—who may not subscribe to it. They may live in fine houses free of mirrors. But I have yet to meet, in any country, such a person. A remarkably prescient twenty-something-year-old might glimpse the situation. After all, she's going to be in it, but, fair enough, it's beyond the majority of people at such an age to engage in this kind of projection.

The question then arises: why in contemporary western society are individuals surprised or indeed, first thing in the morning, toothbrush in hand, alarmed by a face, their own, which once was smooth as a plum but that now resembles a prune? It wasn't always like this. For one thing, there were not as many mirrors, for another people didn't live as long. There weren't avocadoes. There have been societies that equated age with wisdom: the more lined the face, the greater the respect. In a society in which the economy rules and material wealth is the hallmark of status, its older citizens, most of them, no longer productively oiling the economy's cogs, are, unwisely one might quietly suggest, surplus to requirements, a cost. Time on their hands to compose concise epitaphs. This is the serious background.

However, it's the foreground, the face in the mirror, which gives the background a place in the overall picture. It is a very personal encounter, close up as a late self-portrait by an aging Rembrandt. The face in the mirror—not perhaps as remarkably lined as the one we know from photographs of the late W.H. Auden, young Wystan having been erased completely, but lined to a notable degree nevertheless—is the face of someone, typical sooner or later of all who don't cheat by having a surgical procedure, who is yet, if ever, to get used to reaching a significant age. For this particular, though not unique, reason: the face is new. Old, yes, but newly so the older it gets. The only prior experience anyone has of seeing himself in the mirror—or seeing his reflection in a shop window—is when he was younger, which is, up until that point, a whole lifetime. As the wisest members of society know, this goes by unaccountably fast. Psychologically, the bright and indifferent mirror shows, it is a task to keep up.

*

A high-speed long-distance train leaves a station, mid-afternoon, to head north where at the present time of year nightfall is earlier than at this point of departure. On one level every journey is a getting away from oneself, away from those domestic mirrors (memo to self: reduce), he, the passenger sitting next to a window, now thinks. He can recall train journeys when as a child he watched the suburbs give way to green open space; these journeys still refresh him. The train gathers speed. Opposite to him sits a young woman, twenty something, thirty, hard to tell—younger than his own daughters. He looks out attentively at the world through which the train hastens. He himself is all trajectory, once again. Until night, the stealer, surprises him to find his face reflected in the darkened carriage window. He looks away from it, gravely.

ON MEMORY

In memory M. L.

We hadn't met, except in passing on the street, since I gave him the book. Now, as arranged, my friend and I were in a café again, mid-afternoon, in vigorous conversation. It had been a while, two or three years, since we last talked at length, three days now since this last meeting. The beverages were on him, my friend said, in further thanks for the aforementioned book. We were once colleagues in a secondary school and when there was time, during a lunch break perhaps, we'd talk about books. My friend, then the principal of the school, is an avid and informed reader. One year, at the conclusion of the final term, he gave me the *Collected Poems* of Philip Larkin, a new edition, as a Christmas present, having cunningly made certain I didn't already own a copy. I asked him to remind me about the book I had much more recently given to him. He named it, a book with a small print run published by a small publisher, an obscure publication compared to the Larkin, harder to get. Of making this book a gift to my friend, I had no recollection. None.

There is a possibility, I subsequently thought, surprised, no, shocked by this absolute loss of a memory—now that I remember very clearly about this loss made clear in the café—my friend's memory might be the one that is at fault. He had got the book giver wrong. Or, cunning chap, he'd made the whole thing up to test—he was good at giving tests, ask the hundreds of students he'd stood before—how superannuated is the neural network in my brain by setting a trap, so that I might say 'Glad you enjoyed it, a pleasure to get it for you'. Then he'd know, uh oh, I'd failed the memory challenge by admitting to things that had never happened. The problem there is that knowledge (and therefore the gift) of this obscure, small press book published in another country, could realistically only have come via me. In the café, faced with this blank, I found no immediate desire to admit it, diligently sipped my herbal tea (good for restoring one's memory, perhaps) and emerged from this genteel cover-up of a crisis by quickly changing the subject.

Where had that memory gone? From which part of the brain—the hippocampus, say, or the cerebellum—had it vanished? (And why should I have been so surprised? I rarely remember to whom I've lent my books, either.) Somewhere neurotransmission had gone down and was not about to be fixed. A memory gone, a memory of significance—but you have to be reminded, perhaps in a café, that it did once have a source—is akin to a death. I'd challenge any renowned neurologist to shine a light on that damn book, gone missing in my brain, presumed dead, but, sadly, I'd not expect the occasion on which it became a gift to be illuminated. I've tried hard to recover it, with time at my disposal. Nothing doing. Neurologists, those brain experts, truly have their work cut out. Somewhere within 100 billion neurons assisted by 100 trillion synapses, per brain per person, the effective (or ineffective, if damaged) workings of memory exist. That would seem, if viewed spatially, the next thing to an infiniteness—doesn't the mind inhabit the universe?—for things to get lost. A book, for example.

A conflict might complicate the recovery of it: some neuroscientists consider the whole brain inspires memory, others do not. Perhaps annual conferences in Barbados or some other sunny paradise tackle this tricky issue. Perhaps these expert researchers turn their attention to the mind/body problem on their days off. I conclude, in the circumstances, the loss, not of a book itself but the mere memory of giving it seems, many things considered and in the broadest possible perspective, well, nothing much. In any case, it may not be too late for the so-called Proust effect to come into play—as when *In Search of Lost Time* Proust's narrator involuntarily recalls forgotten childhood memories after smelling a wonderful madeleine cake soaked in tea. It may be for me simply a matter getting a beverage, herbal tea, and its sweet accompaniment into sync. Presto! I'll be back in a café bestowing a literary gift.

Writers, one way or another, in works of fiction or of fact, make a pre-emptive strike against oblivion, of which memory loss is a harbinger. Wherever memory may exist. Rupert Sheldrake, the biochemist and author, believes it is inherent in nature, that is, everywhere, a 'morphic field' supplying 'morphic resonance' which, coupled with DNA, makes rabbits rabbits, catfish catfish, and so on and on and on into the mineral world where, if you are lucky, you may find a morphically resonated gem, beautiful in form. I loved the drift of this theory when, many years ago, I listened in a lecture theatre to Sheldrake expounding it, then bought (and continue to buy) his books as much for the beauty of the theory and its applications, providing answers where empirical evidence fails, as for the delightful fact that it can't be proven (or disproven!). The theory floats, untouchable, god-like, in a pure realm. For instance, it provides an explanation as to how termites, say, or ants construct their stunningly complex nests without the aid of an architect—a feat that might make an astonished human gasp. However, we can say, with proven certainty, memory is essential for survival. Otherwise, without the guidance it provides, you might leap into a fire or off a tall building—or permit, with absolute disregard for the obvious consequences, the wholesale felling of the Amazon rainforest, the lungs of the planet, which, strangely, we as a species currently do. Moreover, without memory being in good working order, you might not recognize a long-standing friend.

The café, outside of which I saw him, was not in the same city as the one where I was recently shocked to mislay the memory of a book, though suddenly finding my friend next to me was, about five years ago now, equally surprising. We were both about to cross a road. Fate had dictated this co-incidence much, I suppose, as it had had a chance say in those mandatory freedom-loving days when we attended the same university, handed in assignments late, and mutually tackled the serial hazards of being young. He looked older than when I'd last seen him—a few years earlier, at a book launch—thinner, drawn but I wondered had my appearance so unmistakably changed since the days we quoted the poems of Emily Dickinson ('Because I could not stop for Death /He kindly stopped for me …') and smoked dope? Since he'd stayed, in another state, with my former wife and me on a welcome visit? Since the book launch when I was still a returning visitor to this city upon whose street we both now stood, next to each other, waiting to cross, waiting for the lights to change? When I greeted him, he didn't recognize me. He might have been looking blankly at a cold wall. Until, in the first of many instances, though in this first instance it seemed somewhat absurd, I told him my name. Given name and surname. His face, the face of my old buddy, lit up, no longer estranged.

The large colour photographs, framed, his own, on the walls of his studio were panoramic scenes of inland Australia, the Kimberley especially. He was clearly attracted to expanses and, for distinctive interest, such features as boab trees and huge termite mounds, those structural wonders of the insect world. He had covered a lot of territory, with his cameras and tripod, in his four-wheel drive vehicle. The photographs were a testimony to his patience: his desire to get the mix of shadow and light right. Technically, they looked flawless. Perfect, as they'd proved to be, for corporate boardrooms. Not for him Cartier Bresson's potent 'decisive moment', spontaneity the spur, the captured scene clearly fleeting. No, my friend's photographs, obedient to the golden mean, showed on the one hand little left to chance and on the other his desire to maximize control. They seemed, as I looked at them for the first time, on my first visit to the corner house he and his partner had recently moved into in the inner city, remarkably static. They might have been composed as a hedge against change and forgetfulness.

The studio, as it turned out, was, as a functioning workplace, a pretense—a memorial to an ended career. Though my friend never seemed to admit this to himself, even when, on that first of my many irregular visits, he courageously explained that he had been diagnosed as having a degenerative disease, which I subsequently learned, then further witnessed, affected his memory and spatial awareness. I won't venture into employing clinical terminology, risk a misstep in that contested arena—besides, a specific medical professional's patient was to me not a clinical case but foremost a friend, albeit one I'd not lately seen so often, who on that day we met outside the café had strange trouble explaining to me where he now lived. His days of freely roving were nearly over. The large photographs, so carefully composed and framed behind glass, were stark expressions of his passion for accuracy.

He had, during the last ten or twenty years, made a firm profession out of cheating transience, photography's fixed trick. Now, in a powerful irony, he, not old, was inwardly disappearing.

When the viewing of the studio was over and his partner arrived home from work, back when my friend could still be left at home alone, she—would I recognize this latest?—it comforted me to discover, in the circumstances, recognized me immediately. It was from the book launch, at which I was prominent, since it was my own. I recognized, in time, her forbearance. Eventually, she would tell me—over the ensuing years we engaged in the conversations of the smugly independent—my friend, by now in a hospice, a few weeks ago, had forgotten how to swallow. It had never occurred to me that swallowing was, for adults, unlike breathing, a voluntary act—or had he, in his lostness, not wanted to eat?—that such an unheralded form of memory might be a primary necessity for basic survival. In any case, it remains hard to say when my friend, as a reflective identity, ceased to exist. The photographs, on this matter, remain sharply and brutally in focus.

ON THE RECORD

Foreword

Anecdotes, short though they are, can be revealing—or simply amusing. It's why we trade them in conversation. 'Let me tell you about the time ...' and off you go. They are social currency, conventional in their appeal. Interpretation is not a part of them. Anecdotes litter speeches at weddings and eulogies at funerals. On such occasions the teller assumes some prior knowledge of the person that they are about, takes a short cut to their nub. A lawyer, among a gaggle of lawyers in a pub, equipped with a ready-to-go anecdote about a colleague, should an appropriate opening in conversation occur, will assume those listening will have considerable prior legal knowledge to make the anecdote work. An outsider, listening in, would probably be silently perplexed, she a fine representative of the general public. Anecdotes may be most flexibly effective within tribal boundaries. Nevertheless, for a number I've given an airing over the years, I'm going to assume they have the possibility of a wider life, because they are telling, because they are intrinsically about writers—because when I've told them, more than once on different occasions, I hope not once too often, a hypothetical outsider listening in (drink in hand) may have been a reader, indisputably valued by writers and, in being so, curious to hear a first-hand account in the form of an anecdote about someone in the trade. About a novelist, a poet. That's my justification for preserving them. For the record. For goodness' sake, simply because they are worth telling. One taken at a time, like an analgesic, or two if required.

1

Let me tell you about an incident outlined to me at a bibulous lunch by Morris Lurie. It seemed to Morris instructive, in a delightfully Australian way, about the place of the author in this country. One day, in the seaside town of Mornington, he was in a second-hand bookshop scanning the well-stocked shelves. To his great surprise, he spotted a copy of one of his early novels, a copy of which he no longer possessed. He joyfully extracted it from its second-hand companions, made for the counter, placed the book there, and rested his right hand upon it. Behind the counter stood a young female shop assistant. Morris's eyes met hers. 'I'd like to buy this book', he said, and after a little further thought, pride and an assumed estimation of his status affecting him, he continued, 'I wrote it!'. 'That must have been nice for you', the young assistant flatly responded.

2

Norman MacCaig, the Scottish poet, whose poems are both witty and pithy, was on stage in the big marquee, during an Adelaide Writers Week, in the eighties. I'd spotted him a few days earlier, glass of red wine in hand, sweating profusely in the extreme March heat—poor man, much older than the acclimatized youthful majority—at an opening event for guest writers. This was outside. In direct sunlight he stood, wearing a suit that might have been fine for a cold March day in Scotland. He looked bewildered. Perhaps he'd only that day arrived. Now, in shirtsleeves, standing at ease behind the microphone, standing tall, he introduced and read his poems to an attentive audience, delighted by his Scottish burr. He performed, the audience laughed. Suddenly, somewhere behind him, there was an inexplicable loud bang. MacCaig, retaining his composure, turned away from the audience towards the threat. Nothing obvious to see, he turned back to the microphone. 'Another critic!' he forcefully proclaimed.

3

You wouldn't believe it. Many years ago, while for a few months I was living in Adelaide, I received a phone call from a writer acquaintance. Normally resident in different cities, far apart, we had only met a few times. How he discovered my unlisted phone number, I do not know. Nevertheless, I recognized the voice immediately as belonging to Alan Gould. Apart from, by this time, being published poets, same publisher, of the same age—thirties— we had in common English migrant backgrounds. Alan wondered, since he was in town for a few days, if I would like to join him and a few others for dinner. Certainly, I said. I turned up at the restaurant, sat opposite Alan, and he introduced me to the company. Alan is one of those guys who can quote passages from books with ease. I am impressed by this, having no gift for it. There's a lot, I discovered, as the conversation took priority over the food, less so the drink, that we did not have in common, political sympathies for instance, but no matter. Alan, who to me had a military air that gave him authority, led the conversation. I followed. When, suddenly, I was impressed, no, staggered—my mouth must have stayed open in an O of disbelief—that he could read my mind. He was telepathic. 'Now take Joel Street, Northwood Hills', he'd said, authoritatively, providing it as an illustration for some matter about which we didn't have much in common. 'How', I interrupted, 'did you know I lived there?' That suburban street on the outskirts of Greater London which is inordinately important to me—I've been back to visit it several times—was 12000 miles, on the other side of the earth, from where we were about to approach our ice-cream desserts. Alan stared at me, hard, as if a spell had turned me into a hedgehog. 'I didn't', he slowly replied. 'But how ...' I began. 'That's where I lived', he interposed. Same street, same time, and how uncommon for two boys, who could ride the length of it on a bike in five minutes, never to have connected.

4

When Margaret Scott returned after dark in her car to the Tasman Peninsula, after giving a poetry reading in Hobart or making an ABC television appearance in Sydney or from any number of commitments she agreed to undertake as, late in life, she became ever more popular, a diminutive woman for whom a microphone always had to be lowered so none of her wit would be lost to an audience, she, alone in her car—we could never persuade her to stay in town—would, to keep herself awake, shout 'Elephants! Elephants!' on the long drive home through the marsupial night. She also told, with retrospective disbelief, about her bit part in the newly unfolding drama of one of the most famous literary unions of the twentieth century. She knew first-hand—being back then a Cambridge don—about the night, at a party, Sylvia Plath notoriously bit Ted Hughes on the cheek and drew blood. An unequivocal statement of claim, you might say. Her days, Margaret would state, of offering personal advice of any value were thus about to end. Her best friend was Ted Hughes's current girlfriend. To whom she advised not to worry. 'Oh, he'll come back to you soon enough' she predicated. So too came back time and again—great Scott!— marvellous elephants stampeding out of the dark.

5

Let me tell you about a particular book I have on my shelves. It is Seamus Heaney's debut collection of poetry, *Death of a Naturalist*. First edition, hard cover, dust jacket in good nick, typographical design, now over fifty years old, during which time the late author won the Nobel Prize for Literature. Since, for the moment, I am considering this book as an antiquarian bookseller might as, primarily, an object, whose value, one must hasten to add, is bolstered by its contents and their contribution to the author's oeuvre, the awarding of the big prize enhanced the book as a collectible item. Decades ago, I paid a few dollars for it, wholly for its contents, after I'd spotted it at a second-hand bookstall in an open-air market. Recently, I saw a copy on sale, in a book dealer's glass cabinet, for a four-figure sum. There are variables, no doubt, affecting specific valuations. Here's one. I was introduced to Heaney, a few years before he won the Prize that trounces all others, at a function in his honour while he was visiting Australia. At which time I said, despondently and a tad formally, 'I have a copy of the first edition of your first book which, in my haste, I've neglected to bring along for you to sign'. Heaney replied, sagely, 'You're lucky, you have one of the few copies that isn't'.

6

You choose your children's names carefully. (I recently read about a newborn whose parents wanted to call him Lucifer but the authorities refused to register it.) You examine whether the initials spell a word, or nearly do, that might haunt your kid in the playground. Eventually, you are satisfied that a chosen name, within its cultural context, is fine all round, from all possible viewpoints, and hope for general approval. It isn't always forthcoming. When Tomas Tranströmer, the Swedish poet, visited Tasmania, he had yet, by three decades, to receive the Nobel Prize—the name of the recipient is an annual shock, the judges must be delighted to give to the literary community, which takes twelve months to subside—so Tomas's visit was low-key and that meant I was asked, I forget by whom, to entertain him for an afternoon. Landscape, its breadths and depths, its multiple dimensions, in deep, historical, and personal time, pervades his marvellous poems. If I'd had to pick a distinctive personal quality in him after we'd met I'd have chosen gravity. I decided to take him by the ferry to an island off the coast called Bruny, named after the French explorer Antoine Raymond Joseph de Bruni d'Entrecasteaux, a name his parents must have deliberated over at some length. I had my first daughter with me, aged three. Three years, as a blonde-haired and blue-eyed child, to grow into her much admired name. Tomas politely asked me to tell him it. I was pleased to do so, since it is that of a Norse goddess from his region. 'I expect in your country it's a popular girl's name,' I said, confidently, looking down proudly at my daughter. 'This is Freya.' 'No,' he said gravely, 'this is a name we reserve for dogs and boats.'

7

No matter how wonderful the view from your house, whether it contain the sunlit pyramids of Egypt, a distant smoking volcano surrounded by citrus groves or a cerulean sea with islands visible on the horizon, you will soon become accustomed to it—and if, as a child, you grow up with such a view, it may seem banal from the beginning. When invitations were forthcoming, when Les Murray had already published poems of striking originality and lasting significance, a commonly held view—the word 'visionary' began to be used—I visited him in the unremarkable Sydney suburb of Chatswood, though he and his family had in their back garden, I recall, a rampant *Monstera deliciosa,* the largest and most wonderful specimen I'd ever seen. It was nothing special to them. By this time, Les, the curmudgeon, whose friends one day are to him his enemies the next—what better way to keep one's views of fellow humans refreshed—was rightly beginning to be seen as a future candidate for the Nobel Prize. The judges may yet surprise his admirers and make the name Les Murray glow afresh. That day of my first visit, first book newly published, his young daughter, Clare, was home from school, and while Les, soon after I arrived, answered the phone, I idly asked a question, stunned by how daft it was as soon as I'd uttered it. 'What's your dad been up to?' I enquired. 'Oh, just writing poems,' she brightly replied.

8

I once lived above a newsagent's shop owned by a man known to his many loyal customers as the Mayor. If anyone wanted specific local knowledge or wished to trade some gossip, he was their man, an affable, loquacious, smart Kenyan-born Indian. The shop was in Belsize Park, north London, and he'd run it for as long as anyone could remember, after migrating to the UK. He'd stand behind his counter, a man of influence, beaming a welcoming smile. He told me that one day, one dreary, wet day, Beryl Bainbridge had been in the shop. He recognized her, not because he'd read any of her novels and studied the author photo, but because he'd seen her picture many times in the paper. He knew, because I had told him, that I was at the time bingeing on Bainbridge's novels, had just read the wickedly funny *Injury Time,* set in the area. Dame Beryl, late in her life, was viewed as a chain-smoking eccentric with a liking for drink. She, a former actress who had appeared in *Coronation Street,* played up to this view—the mischief in her shrewd novels played out in life—and indeed in contemporary photos in her final decade she looks raddled. Thus, she appeared in the shop, in a raincoat, wet through, and made past the glossy magazines to the counter. It was then, or shortly after—she had not been in the shop before, although she lived locally—that the Mayor recognized her as the famous author. However, he saw immediately her face was badly bruised. 'Have you had a fall? he enquired, sympathetically, before she'd had a chance to buy a packet of fags. 'No,' she said, 'I was mugged.' Maybe the Mayor thought he'd missed the story in the papers; I thought, as he told it to me, of corresponding events in *Injury Time*. 'Did the mugger,' the Mayor cautiously ventured, 'take anything?' Her reply was steady: 'Yes, he took my Rolex watch.' From her skinny wrist, her face soon to grace the obituaries. 'But,' she added, deadpan, 'it didn't matter. The watch was a fake.'

9

Let me tell you about a particular kind of elective surgery: vasectomy. Here, since I don't have the anatomical knowledge of a surgeon, is the definition in my old *Chambers Dictionary*: 'Vasectomy (Gr. Ek, out, tomē, a cut), excision of the vas deferens, or part of it, esp. in order to produce sterility'. The vas deferens, by the way, is a spermatic duct. What this doesn't tell you, and I had first-hand knowledge of this after I decided that fathering more children would be irresponsible (still, I liked to think, in my prime), is that the procedure, under a local anesthetic, is overshadowed by a lot of grim counselling. What if your children are killed in a car crash? Etc etc. In spite of this, I optimistically decided to proceed. Something else the dictionary definition cannot possibly touch upon is that if you have a vasectomy in a hospital in a small town, in my case in Hobart, Tasmania, where no matter what one's best efforts have been to avoid media attention, it has failed, the procedure might spur in you, the patient, a powerful desire to move somewhere else where anonymity is king. Stretched out on a trolley, an orderly wheeled me into the operating theatre where I'd have my third and final anesthetic, before, under the bright lights, work would begin. The anesthetist there, new to me, an attractive woman belonging to my generation, removed a white towel so that my shaved parts were no longer private, jabbed the needle in, at which time the surgeon, a well-spoken man of senior years, studied his instruments, and soon began what for him was routine, what for me was life changing. In spite of the doses of anesthetic, I felt some minor discomfort. My eyes must have betrayed this, the anesthetist's attention having drifted away from the procedure I was glad, being supine, not to be witnessing. 'Aren't you the poet?' she asked, innocently, as her brown eyes met mine.

10

Gwen, Gwennie, as she might sign off a letter, Gwendoline, the name on her birth certificate, but I only ever knew her use no-nonsense Gwen. She would not suffer fools. Awe, at the mention of the name Gwen Harwood, the name she used for her poetry, was, when I first knew her, the standard response. Only 16% of Nobel laureates for literature have been women—what an outrage!—so she probably never gave the prospect a thought. By then it was well known she had notoriously used in the past an array of, mostly male, pseudonyms. My initial chance at getting a sense of this remarkable woman was in my new role as the young editor of a literary magazine in which Gwen would regularly publish. Late one afternoon she launched its first edition, a task she had generously agreed to perform though I, having previously only met her fleetingly (I was new in town) didn't arrange it. That afternoon was bitterly cold and wet, mid-winter in Tasmania and, it now being late, growing dark, house and streetlights were already punctuating it. A southerly wind battered the van—it was exemplary Gothic weather—that carried the magazine editors, the magazine launcher and, in their boxes, the magazines. Gwen, sitting quietly next to me, eyes front, seemingly undistracted by the squeaky windscreen wipers doing their active best, suddenly venomously exclaimed, 'This place is evil!' I'd heard she had a low opinion of the island and its violent history (it was her husband's decision to live there) but expressed in a breathless, high-pitched, exasperated voice this exclamation seemed, out of nowhere, on the way to welcome a new magazine into the world, a devastating assessment. Still, we drove on. The short woman who soon after stepped into the role of launcher, in a large private house, wore a long-sleeved floral dress open at the neck. To me, thirty years her junior, she looked like someone's kindly, forgiving aunt. She said many kind things about the new magazine in her girlish, gentle voice. Where had her double suddenly gone? In spite of the fact that the room was crowded, it was cold; there was a fireplace but not, through some lapse in planning, a fire. This a young woman who lived in the house was by now attending to, crouched, striking matches, adjusting the wood, blowing hard, desperate. Gwen went over to inspect. I edged closer, drink in hand, kind of expectant. A little smoke, of no consequence, rose. I was soon relieved Gwen's public estimation, in her launch speech, of the magazine (still airborne, dear Gwen, almost forty years later) did not in any way echo her private reckoning of the attempt she witnessed to make fire. 'How pathetic!' I heard her say, with the force of her earlier exclamation, not quite under her breath. Then, without any further comment, Gwen made her exit from the event.

Afterword

Ten, that's it, a suitably round number. Should I venture further into double figures with more anecdotes I'd be in danger of corralling living writer friends—with fine sensibilities—into the gathering. This would not do. Let me tell you, these are highly articulate, well-connected people who know, if necessary, how to exact revenge. I value their friendships. It is also a shocking and marvellous truth that I wouldn't know where to dare to begin.

ON SMOKING AND SOCIAL ATOMISATION

Smoking gets people out of their houses, if they are smokers. Or perhaps if they're not. Let me provide an example relating to a smoker, one of the social lepers of our time. I have a neighbour, a prominent collector of art as it happens, a single man whose companion is a dog—young dog, man of senior years—who lives in a Victorian terrace house, small front garden, iron fence, the gate opening directly onto the street. On that gate, shut, he leans and smokes. A cheerful consequence of this, weather permitting, is that during the course of a day when he goes out from his house to lean and muse and smoke he will soon enough find himself in verbal engagement with a passer-by: a near neighbor, a distant acquaintance, a fellow dog lover or a more general, sociable other. I am, fortunately, one of these people and as a consequence have learned a few things about Australian art that I didn't know before, some nice insider stuff. Before long the cigarette has burned down to the filter and is, I've noticed, not replaced by another no matter how long the conversation. Smokers are increasingly few, non-smokers increasingly many and—I'm guessing—this neighbor of mine is therefore reckoning that on average bordering on certainty he's talking to a non-smoker and doesn't want to sign off in the air, abruptly, a conversation with an impressive signature of smoke, he an addicted victim, some might say, of the tobacco industry. Non-smokers, whose olfactory sense is as radar to the regime of a threatened country, are fast to read the danger, the telegraphed health warning that arrives via a lit cigarette. Cowed smokers, in affluent suburbs, who know the health of the whole planet is for other reasons seriously failing, are sympathetic and lay off.

This art collector isn't compelled to get out of his house to enjoy a cigarette; his dog won't bite him if to do so he stays inside. Perhaps when the wind is keen and the rain diagonal he does. I don't know. There's often hardly anything we do know about our neighbours as they come and go, nothing, perhaps, except the make of their car if they're from a few doors down, chronically alone maybe, but who knows, as a house, one day a home, becomes real estate the next, the for sale or for lease sign abruptly up, then soon the removal van is slowly pulling out with its full load, money the driver of everything. Remarkable to think of new apartment blocks, developments speedily erected, with enough inhabitants to fill a large village, full from top to bottom with strangers. In each block a featureless lift, the artery, resembling a leafy main road only in the sense that all of its inhabitants take it—but never, in any meaningful way, connect. Welcome to atomized living. So well established one might assume it's widely welcome. Unlike cigarette smoke. I bet there are NO SMOKING signs everywhere and in all of them—and anti-smoking campaigners. And so, I have noticed, outside an apartment block I drive past, in all possible weathers and at a regulated distance from the entrance, shelter a possible option, there are guilty smokers, companions in exile and, undeniably welcome, they are talking to each other—even, in the shadow of the building, forming bonds as in a small nascent society, a rascally fleeting utopia hooked on an anachronistic drug.

His own option being his iron front gate, my neighbor, a patient man it seems to me, watches as does a fisherman from a riverbank for his float to disappear in deep water and signal a potential catch. He, in his chosen or accepted solitude, will soon have something to say to a passer-by—smoking, the anti-social habit, becoming a social conduit. Without evidence to the contrary, he may well have calculated or assumed with fair certainty that I am not a smoker. I'm guessing. I don't know—don't know much, as is usual about one's neighbours. The boundary between art and personal habits has, mercifully, not been crossed in our conversations, whether at his gate, the cigarette dwindling, or elsewhere on a street, should I run into him, where until further restrictions to smoking are imposed on public spaces, it's still OK for him to smoke.

There was once, he'd remember, an accepted etiquette to smoking. In the street, at a party, or in a pub when smokers were many and health warnings were few, it was a courtesy to offer companions or a new acquaintance, possibly a desirable member of the opposite sex, a cigarette. Then, perhaps seductively, offer a light. A cigarette was not just the provider of a nicotine hit, it was a social gift. I record this aspect of our cultural history before it is hygienically cleansed from memory. Unlamented now windows are no longer left open with the prime purpose of clearing the air of tobacco smoke. Or kept inconsiderately shut.

So there was a time within diminishing memory when justifiably sensitive non-smokers stepped outside with relief into the fresh air—and possibly garnered the advantages this confers on smokers today, such as my neighbour, the collector of art and receiver of conversation. The acrid smell of ready-made cigarettes drove them out. This sensitivity I sympathised with and understood. It was to my mind, since I well remember those days, a discriminating move when other lethal threats were harder to banish, such as the pressing global threat of nuclear war. In other interiors, the ones I grew up in, it was pipe smoke, my father's, which influenced air quality, the tobacco extracted from vacuum sealed tins. Specifically, St Bruno Roughcut when we lived in London, then swapped, after a brief lament, for Erinmore Mixture in distant Melbourne, a discriminating immigrant's compromise choice. These tobaccos were not aromatic and nor was their smell, like that of a Marlboro or other ready-mades, acrid. Who'd smoke them! The smoke of the pipe tobacco smelled, to the best of my knowledge, like home. It didn't drive me out to pass the time where frustrated non-smokers did once and smokers do now, advantageously, as I say. For instance, stepping out at night to see, coincidentally and with delight, a tawny frogmouth perched on a telegraph wire or, some other time, a ringtail possum, joey clinging to her back, going rapidly along it. Or stepping out from a tightly inhabited cabin in a national park, and seeing other creatures of the night, say, a spotted quoll in a clearing—and away from the city lights, countless stars and many meteorites. For which, of course, the assistance of a cigarette is as unnecessary as it may be necessary for a man to solicit conversation while leaning on an iron gate. To all of this I am a witness—and as for discriminating between cigarette types I, with decreasing frequency but still with attendant pleasure, nocturnally inhabit the home verandah, briefly exiled from those indoors, have a glass of whisky and roll my own.

ON MORTALITY

On this day as I write, when I was a boy over fifty years ago, my mother took her own life. Where would we be without an agreed-upon calendar? The Babylonian, the Zoroastrian, the Hellenic, the Julian ... we eventually settled on the Gregorian calendar, we being those of us who live in the West. Or rather, at the outset, Pope Gregory X111 did it for us. The reason? For which day of the year was it? It was to regularize the annual date for Easter, the day of Christ's resurrection from the dead. The first known calendar dates back to the Bronze Age when, perhaps by firelight, definitely by supreme calculation, there was a desire to get some firm ritualized order into unpredictable pagan life. My mother, a Christian, took to regularly going to church during the last months of her life. Unlike my father, she was a believer. Easter for me was chocolate eggs time, a side issue for her. She went on Sunday mornings to her source of comfort, the church, without my father or, for that matter, me. I'd sometimes go to meet her on the street, on her way back home. On the day of rest before consumerism made a final successful assault upon it.

It was on a Sunday that she took an overdose of barbiturates, emptied their brown jar, several days before my twelfth birthday, my first in Australia. Different country, same reliable calendar. The fateful Sunday was also the birthday of one of my cousins back in England. He recently told me while I was visiting him, that the phone call his mother, my mother's sister, received in Manchester from my father in Melbourne, to tell her what had happened, ruined his eleventh birthday. It was a right piss-off, he said. So it is a day for him to remember too and, with an unaccountable laugh, I could belatedly sympathise with the fact that his birthday celebrations had taken a bit of a hit. A weeping woman has no place next to a birthday cake with eleven candles aflame.

Since that Sunday, those many decades ago, and I think I'm being as accurate as the 365 days on the annual calendar will allow, on the dozens of calendars that have been binned during my life, not one day has slipped by when I haven't thought a little or a lot about my mother. Not so much about the circumstances of her death, the drama, no, that's another matter entirely, but about her. This is, since I am not a believer, her afterlife. It was an act of courage, I have always thought, that gave her this, especially in view—and especially then—of the church's insitutionalised attitude towards suicide. Am I typical, in my daily involuntary remembrance, of those who have suffered the death of a mother they were close to when young? When she appears in my dreams, as occasionally she still does, she is a lot younger than I am now, which is a fine and fabulous state of affairs; it puts her at a youthful advantage to me. In which case it is her not specifically me who is arrested in time, if one chose to say such a thing of a typical person shocked to the core by a loss, though it wasn't immediate, and who began to become so on that Sunday long, long ago. A bit of a kid, companion in perpetuity to a parental absence, in a now visibly ageing body, whose own departure, dissolution, death on a day and date, alliterative momentum notwithstanding, is yet to be reckoned, but nevertheless with a perfect right of place on a calendar, as having been assigned that particular merit.

There is a good reason why William Shakespeare's lines in *Hamlet* about the metaphorical prospect after death as being 'The undiscovered country from whose bourn/no traveler returns' are among his most famous. We can bet on a lot of things that are going to happen—which frog will hop the furthest, which book will win the Booker Prize—but not what happens or, more to the point, where we go after we die. There's a good deal of disagreement about this. One person in the bet is not going to be around to pay or collect. So the bets are off. Hamlet is prone to delaying tactics, Michel de Montaigne, in his *Essays*, digression. Shakespeare it seems read him closely and no doubt came across this apposite observation for those, most of us, reluctant to face up to mortality:

> … live as long as you can, you shall be nothing shorter
> the space you are dead; it is all to no purpose: you shall
> be every whit as long in the condition you so much fear,
> as if you had died at nurse …

The Roman poet philosopher, Lucretius, who from antiquity speaks as freshly to us now, like a friend, as he did to Montaigne—this is an elite bunch of scribes we're bringing to the matter at hand—is similarly pragmatic, wonderfully sanguine, in making a corresponding point, and at a clip:

> The life of mortals has a limit set to it, my friend.
> Death has no loopholes. All of us must meet it in the end.
> …
> No one knows what the years to come will bring—what joy or strife
> May lie in store for us, what outcome's looming in our lot.
> But by adding on to life, we don't diminish by one jot
> The length of death, nor are we able to subtract instead
> Anything to abbreviate the time that we are dead.

Though centuries have passed, and we now have such wonders as the mobile phone to keep in touch with the living, what these (immortal) writers have nailed will not be revolutionized in time, ever, to accommodate the universally applied delaying tactics of every last one of us marked out for the reaper, that is, unless we choose to take the matter into our own hands. Our ingenuity has its limits. 'Death', Lucretius says elsewhere in *The Nature of Things*, 'is nothing to us; it concerns us not a jot,/seeing we hold the mind is mortal'. Lucretius, like Epicurius before him—whose philosophy Lucretius approvingly absorbed—is an atomist and atomists contend that atoms are all in the universe there is. Death is a full stop. However not for my aunt, my mother's sister, the aforementioned birthday spoiler.

That small, spry, forceful woman has been representative in my life, since hers so often played a part in mine, of the many humans, perhaps the world's majority, who believe in a hereafter. She knew where she stood during her mortal journey: on one side of another life. She observed in church the Christian calendar exactly. She also had a supremely keen ear for blasphemy. As a boy, I was in dangerous proximity to her when, in response to some surprise, perhaps birdshit landing on my shoulder from a passing seagull, I uttered the word 'Crikey!' This was on a joint family holiday, in which my aunt played the dominant role, played out in one of those vintage coastal villages in England. I was yet to tower over her in height, so that the back of my head was an easy target for the palm of her hand. The force of it hitting me made me fall forward—impressive but it didn't come with any explanation. It was very much later that I discovered my irreverent exclamation was a slang contraction of 'Christ help me', though my aunt and I never followed up the incident with an etymological discussion of the word or, indeed, any other word. There are mysteries other than those concerning the hereafter: now I'll never know since I neglected to ask how or where she got the arcane lowdown on that word—perhaps a tipoff from a priest—for it is into the hereafter she now has gone. It took her ninety-five years to achieve it. The little bruiser had by then, and many years before, to all appearances become like a bespectacled sweet old lady in a sentimental movie, her late husband, my uncle, a bit of a quandary. For how, she wondered aloud to me one time, still lucidly, in her nursing home in Somerset, was she going to recognize him in, I presumed, heaven after all those years since he'd died. She appeared to imagine that without her energetic attentions he'd now look like an unkempt, longhaired tramp. I wish for her, bless her, wherever she might have found him, the possession of a comb.

My aunt never in this connection, thankfully, mentioned my mother. Back among the living where death may be nothing to us—like the atomists, I don't expect to bump into anyone on the other side, unkempt or not—doesn't mean that mortality isn't grounds for specific lamentation. I looked in the bathroom mirror this morning, shaving brush in hand, and again saw a man I wouldn't have recognized as the reverse spitting image of me a mere decade or two ago. He is called, so those who on Melbourne public transport are younger may verbally identify him and respectfully give up their seat, a senior. Just let them try. Guess who will lament it. Montaigne, equable, all inclusive—thus embracing those early discoverers of mortality, a subset of public transport users, youth—states: 'To lament that we shall not be alive a hundred years hence, is the same folly as to be sorry we were not alive a hundred years ago'. Good advice for the young, good advice for the old. In any case, personal extinction is a microscopic matter—minute individual, huge universe—but no less hugely significant for being so, since we only get one go at being personally extinguished, in the face of general entropy: leading eventually, though fortunately beyond any relevance now or a hundred or a thousand years hence, to the dying sun cooling and the earth on a trajectory toward oblivion. As they say on the windows of shops that are soon to close down, and which always seems to me to be an all-embracing but unnecessary metaphysical reminder, 'EVERYTHING MUST GO'. Thus it is never too late, thinks the defiant man or woman on their last legs, to get that ultimate pair of shoes on the cheap. Or, for that matter, next year's necessary calendar.

ON THE FUTURE

There is evidence for the existence of the past but none of the future. The past is as weighty as the samples of rock I have on display in the room where I write—gneiss, scoria, limestone, schist, for example, and a marvelous chunk of petrified wood; the permineralisation of the latter began about twenty million years ago. There, for all in the present to see, is proof of the rings annually formed in a tree, buried by volcanic ash. It would make, should I ever need one, a great doorstop. Each rock contains a story of its past, origins in deep time, ready for any rock lover to discover. The spherical scoria, which I found on a shingle beach in Turkey, is evidence of a long since extinct volcano. However when the scoria flew out of it, during an eruption, there was no evidence of what would become of the pleasingly egg-shaped rock—a pleasure, after I spotted it, to toss from hand to hand. Yet, wonder of wonders, here it is on a table a hemisphere away—who could predict it?—millions of years on from where, with a lot of accompanying magma, it shot up into the wide blue sky, if the sun was out, if the eruption was during the day and not the night, neither of which, if we heed Ludwig Wittgenstein, might necessarily recur. 'It is an hypothesis', he wrote, 'that the sun will rise tomorrow: and this means that we do not know whether it will rise'. This is a point, made by a pre-eminent philosopher, that no-one whose savings are locked up in an account accruing compound interest can ignore. There's no hard evidence (a certain probability, yes) that its sunny date of maturity, say on a Wednesday, will actually, shadows and all, ever happen.

Many years ago, that is in the verifiable past, I strongly sympathized with young Tess in Thomas Hardy's great novel *Tess of the D'Urbervilles* when with foreboding she says, "You seem to see numbers of tomorrows just all in a line, the first of them biggest and clearest, the others getting smaller and smaller as they stand further away; but they all seem very fierce and cruel as if they said, 'I'm coming! Beware of me! Beware of me!'" As we know, fate for Tess, in the form of the gallows, eliminated that prospect. However, we, the readers, live on, grow older, no longer worry so, and indeed might repeat that tomorrow never comes, at least in the form of a tomorrow, which is in the future, and that it barely involves a verbal sleight of hand to say therefore that, on the weight of evidence, its existence is a continuously questionable matter. Only someone with rocks in his head would conceivably spend time thinking about an actual future. What's the point?

The future is forever beyond cognition, except as an abstract. For those of us who see the world in a concrete manner, it's nothing particular. In terms of chronology, the present is the paradoxical continuous end of events. On a daily basis, I employ the future tense but this involves an act of faith. Like palmistry. Like astrology. The practitioners of these arts can say what they like about the future, your unique, precious one and only future, because they can. There are no reality checks out there where fate can declare itself foreseen.

For the past, I have respect. We may learn something from it. For the present, I have a suggestion: that I will continue to live in it. For the future ... I will disparage it no more, except to say it over occupies many of us when we cannot ever occupy it. I would, of course, flee a forest fire and make for the open to live another day. Or shoot a fox that attacks the chickens which will supply tomorrow's eggs. In more customary circumstances, when I have satisfied my considerable appetite for the present by, for example, shifting my gaze from my rock collection to witness, today, early signs of spring outside the window, the buds, the blossom, the blue cloudless sky, I may, as I did yesterday, on a whim, open an old family photograph album—yesterday the weather was dreary—and give the frozen images therein my vital regard, a regard for the past. There, looking at the camera and, by extension, seemingly looking at me, in various poses, colluders in the trick of the photograph, were forebears of mine. For a number of them, since they had died before I was born, though they were then very much alive on a promenade, a beach, next to a pavilion—summer has drawn these folk out from English suburbia—I have to rely on the dubious veracity of black and white photographs to get some kind of measure of them, while they were out and about putting on their best facial expressions for the photographer. For posterity, the future. That's where I come in, albeit briefly on a dreary afternoon, utterly beyond their ken: I will not possibly exist, it's beyond any imagining when, in their day, summer hubris in play, they most certainly do. Nothing to it, really.